A

BRITISH

NIGERIAN

"DEADBEAT"

IN

CINCINNATI

Charles Chuka Aniagolu

Order this book online at www.trafford.com
or email orders@trafford.com

Most Trafford titles are also available at major online book retailers.

Note for Librarians: A cataloguing record for this book is available from Library
and Archives Canada at www.collectionscanada.ca/amicus/index-e.html

Printed in Victoria, BC, Canada.

ISBN: 978-1-4251-8858-0 (sc)

*We at Trafford believe that it is the responsibility of us all, as both individuals
and corporations, to make choices that are environmentally and socially sound.
You, in turn, are supporting this responsible conduct each time you purchase
a Trafford book, or make use of our publishing services. To find out how you
are helping, please visit www.trafford.com/responsiblepublishing.html*

*Our mission is to efficiently provide the world's finest, most comprehensive book publishing
service, enabling every author to experience success. To find out how to publish your
book, your way, and have it available worldwide, visit us online at www.trafford.com*

Trafford rev. 10/21/2009

 www.trafford.com

North America & international
toll-free: 1 888 232 4444 (USA & Canada)
phone: 250 383 6864 ♦ fax: 250 383 6804 ♦ email: info@trafford.com

The United Kingdom & Europe
phone: +44 (0)1865 487 395 ♦ local rate: 0845 230 9601
facsimile: +44 (0)1865 481 507 ♦ email: info.uk@trafford.com

Contents

TO

JACQUI, JACINTA AND JOSHUA

"And then they were three…"

For

THERESA & YASMIN

PART ONE

(Caveat Viator: Let The Traveller Beware)

ATLANTA

Wednesday, 10ᵗʜ May 2000, crack of dawn.

A damp rigorous cold had fogged up southern England and the region was almost lost from sight beneath a condensed drizzle of water droplets and ice crystals.

Glimpsing the obscuring mist from his three-bedroom flat in north London, Peter Oti winced. The weather had turned unmercifully inclement. Dark brooding clouds, heaving with precipitation, massed across the sky, casting a tempestuous shadow over the suburb of Golders Green where Peter lived, enveloping everything in a cheerless grey and plunging temperatures into the single digits.

It was May but the seasons had clearly mixed it up, said the weedy bespectacled meteorologist on BBC Breakfast News. Spring was yet to strike. The normally smooth, if slightly rocky, transition from the winter solstice to the vernal equinox had taken an unexpectedly rough turn. The sun had been vanquished by a sudden volley of furious storms, reduced to a grey-blue luminescence and banished south.

The re-empowered winter sky glowed darkly in triumph. Its grip regained, the coldest season of the year became wayward and intractable, commanding arctic storms to torment the inhabitants of the British Isles. The thunderclouds they drove were wrought with turbulence, chilly with ice.

Under normal circumstances, Peter's mood would have plunged. He resented the punishment of winter – the endless darkness, the cold constant rain, the despondency and longing for natural heat.

But circumstances were not normal today and unusually for Peter the freezing wind and angry storm mattered not so much as a boiled bean. He felt so utterly hot. Not even the terrible gloom unleashed by this *winter-morning-in-the-middle-of-May-for-God's-sake* turn of weather could diffuse his mood of warm vigorous elation.

Peter had risen with the first light of dawn, which meant that on this wintry morning it was seven thirty. He had packed his suitcase the previous night and was dressed and waiting when the pre-booked minicab from the office near Hendon Central tube station with the telephone number ending in *666* arrived dead on 8.00, driven by a pot-bellied, middle-aged Nigerian cabbie with tiny, almost invisible ears and a huge upper lip. The all-new *666* mini-cab service, with the Pillsbury Doughboy at the wheel, only larger and darker, thought Peter.

That would make him the fifth minicab driver in a row of Nigerian extraction that had come to ferry Peter to various work-related assignments in the past fortnight. Recently, Peter had read with much doubt a newspaper article suggesting that anywhere between eight hundred thousand and three million Nigerians could be living in the UK – many of them underground -- with around a quarter in London. Now as he passed his things on to the portly cabbie to be loaded into his aging Ford Mondeo, it occurred to Peter aloud that the article might have some kernel of truth after all.

"Well, counting British born Nigerians, plus legal and illegal immigrants, that figure could well be right", said the chatty cab driver, the thick slice of his upper lip rising and falling densely. His name was Ola, short for Olaudah.

"I have the special honour of being named after one of the most famous British Igbo Nigerians, Olaudah Equiano, a former slave who lived in the UK in the 17th Century and who became a prominent member of the British slave trade abolition movement".

Boy was Ola the cabbie chatty. Peter learned within a couple of minutes that he was born and raised in Benin, capital of Edo state in mid-western Nigeria, an area of great civilisation that once formed part of a large, pre-colonial African kingdom known as Benin Empire that flourished between the 14th and 19th centuries, but which today was rather notorious internationally for being the largest exporter of prostitutes from West Africa to Western

Europe. An ancient, powerful kingdom, that rose, sunk back and became lost in the tropical vegetation, swallowed by time.

"I am part of the X generation of Nigerians scattered all over the world, living in misery because our *wayo* (corrupt) leaders at home have collapsed our country", he said, smiling bitterly, eyeing Peter through his rear view mirror. "I was not lucky enough to be a so-called British Nigerian because I was born in Africa. So even though I have a masters degree, I am driving taxi here in London".

He glanced at Peter as they inched forward through rush hour traffic.

"Are you Nigerian?"

"I am", Peter said, then added as an afterthought, "*British Nigerian*".

That didn't seem to impress him much.

"Which tribe are you from?"

Peter hated that word *tribe*. It sounded so ancient, so aboriginal, evoking unwelcome visions in his mind's eye of primitive clans of autochthonous pre-literate peoples wearing palm leaf skirts and grinning Sambo-like out of black and white photographs. "If you mean what part of Nigeria are my parents from, they are from the east", Peter replied evenly.

"Aah", said the cab driver with a sarcastic, gruff laugh. "So you are one of those who distance themselves from their African roots. It is not where you are from but where your parents are from, eh?"

Peter didn't like the way the conversation was going. The fellow sounded discourteous and blunt, threatening to shift Peter's mood from euphoria to something rather more tart, reminding him of things he didn't want to be reminded of, certainly not on this day. Things like his struggle with his sense of cultural identity, the feeling that he would never fully fit into either British or Nigerian society, that it wasn't just Nigerians born in Nigeria, but also white people, and that Indian fellow called Nim from the five-ways corner shop who reminded Peter of some kind of burrowing animal and who, when he told them he was British, responded brusquely, "yeah, but where are you originally from?" or in some cases, "where are you *really* from?"

Which was why the Foreign Office under Tony Blair's government had come up with the perfect term "British Nigerian", to describe people like Peter who were born on the British Isles of Nigerian parentage. Thanks to that stroke of inventive semantic genius, the likes of Peter could legitimately claim dual identity, without compromising one for the other and without being mocked.

In any case, he didn't want to discuss any of it with fat garrulous lips here. Peter was still dreaming large and images of the epic quest he was about to embark on were firing his soul. He was not going to ruin the mood by bucking heads with some rambling, blubber-faced cabbie. So Peter grunted "Of course not" in reply, closed his eyes and pretended to fall asleep.

Through storm clouds and wedges of crammed traffic – Finchley Road cutting through St John's Wood, then Marble Arch and down Park Lane – the Nigerian cabbie, having no one to engage in blusterous conversation, concentrated on hastening his Ford Mondeo to Victoria Station, where they arrived twenty-five minutes later. Peter bid him a cheerful farewell and caught the Gatwick Express, a shuttle train service with tourist bright railway carriages, operating non-stop between Victoria and Gatwick airport about 50 miles away.

They raced past train stations and faceless people waiting on rain swept platforms and a convoy of military vehicles loaded with munitions and endless rows of grim looking council blocks and quaint mock Tudors.

The train arrived thirty minutes later and Peter alighted. He stood for a moment at the bottom of the escalator and looked around. Crowds of people of every hue, laden with luggage, were squeezing into the narrow escalating stairwell, then welling up from the circulating belt like a spring from a fountain. Where do

all these people come from and where are they going, he wondered momentarily?

Peter joined the great tide of bodies. He was travelling light as
usual with only his briefcase and a small Salopian portmanteau,
which slipped right into the space beside him. You couldn't walk
half a metre to the left or right without colliding with someone
or something.

Weaving through hundreds of travellers, Peter spent sixty irritating minutes queuing and checking in at the British Airways
desk and another twenty passing through immigration and security. Then he turned into the departure lounge.   The place was
packed with people escaping from winter's late surge, heading for
the hot sands and seas of the Mediterranean and the Americas.

Peter paid for a mug of over-priced hot chocolate and with
some difficulty found a seat facing away from the bank of flight
monitors so that he had to turn his neck almost one hundred and
eighty degrees to read what was on those screens.

There was no urgency for the moment. He had thirty minutes to blow before he would have to make his way down to the
boarding gate. So he sat back and relaxed his mind, sipping the
steaming chocolate. It was delicious, made the way a chocolate
beverage was meant to be prepared, entirely with hot fresh milk
rather than hot water with a dash of powdered milk, as they did
back in the home country.

Everything felt pleasantly mellow, rather like a warm sunny
spring day. A world bursting into ostentatious florescence, kicking with pleasurable effect, one of the finest days in his entire life,
full of promise and dazzle.

Peter had excellent reason to flap his wings. Every nerve in
his body, every sinewy muscle reminded him so completely of the
immediate future that awaited him. He was on his way to sign-
ing a lucrative contract as news anchor with CNN International.
Working in such a high profile job with the so-called world's news
leader, was a dream he coveted above all else. Patiently, he had
nurtured it for several years, variously as news presenter, corre-

spondent, reporter and producer with the BBC, ITN and Sky News, barrelling past equally ambitious competitors, dodging political bullets whilst doing a fair bit of grovelling and arse licking, until at last, the time had come, as he hoped it would.

Peter thought of the thousands of journos and TV punters ("lens lice" as they were called in the business) across the globe that would kill to be in his position. But as good ol' fate would have it, by a decree of destiny, it was Peter Oti that fortune had seen it fit to bestow this singular honour upon. He had done it, broken through, slaked his driving ambition on the set of the world's most watched news network, the tower of awesome tele-visual power. It was like wrestling with a mighty dragon, and though the beast had ducked and dived for a while he had eventually brought it to heel, leashed it in his grasp. He had stared down the greatest medium of the millennium in the year of the millennium.

And now, having passed through the breath of flames, he had entered the dragon and was plugged into the mains bubble. He could feel the power surging all around him, coursing through his veins, elevating him to levels of tele-journalistic fame hardly imaginable to most people. He felt giddy with exhilaration.

Shortly after 11.30am, Peter boarded the British Airways jet bound for Atlanta Georgia.

The plane was full to bursting. Peter was glad he was in business class. Back in economy, people were squeezed together rather like workers in an ant colony. Peter saw a group of grossly overweight Americans of all shades – some kind of group booking -- battling their way into the nest, armed with their hand luggage, forcing their way through, fitting their vast backsides into the narrow wedge of world traveller seating.

Peter felt for the flight attendants who had the job of ministering to them. The two airhostesses in his line of vision looked about them with the fixed smiles and poker faces of European professionals. But underneath, if you were observing things as keenly as Peter was, you would surely detect the subtle movement of anguished eyes, the soft sighs that betrayed nervousness as more very loud, very large American passengers bulked their way into economy class. Imagine having to serve that lot, who sounded like a most coarse-mannered, self-indulgent bunch. They were sure to assail you with irritating requests for all kinds of peddler stuff. Insisting querulously and at the top of their lungs on their rights, with a vigorous shaking of their fat heads and much waving of their substantial arms.

Somehow the exasperated attendants managed to settle everyone and put their hand luggage away. Twenty-five minutes later the engines of the Airbus roared into life and the plane lifted off. As it strove to gain altitude, Peter looked out the window at the leaden sky and down at the misted houses twinkling with lights and spread out in every direction. He felt like Gulliver the giant towering over the diminutive inhabitants of Lilliput who were wandering around way down beneath.

The aircraft headed out through the fog. Peter could just make out the foaming coastline and a distant curve that might have been the white cliffs of Dover. The jet finished executing a long bumpy turn. Peter watched engrossed as the earth turned into a blurry picture of a satellite relief map and disappeared.

The roar of the engines eased. Peter closed his eyes. He was glad the journey had finally begun. He was competitive and impatient and hated waiting for anything – a life dominated by a strict, hugely ambitious father, who wanted to mould Peter in his own image, had seen to that. One month of hanging about for meetings to be arranged with CNN executives had tested Peter severely. Had they made a terrible omission and forgotten about him? He sat close to the phone everyday, hoping they would ring as promised, his heart throbbing with anxiety and excitement. But weeks came and went without a word, leaving him feeling dejected and unfulfilled. When finally they called a month and a half later with flight and hotel bookings, Peter felt exultant relief. He was back in his element. It was a supreme moment in the glowing career of Peter Oti.

Peter had already made several presenting appearances on

CNN International delivering the evening and early morning bulletins to millions of viewers around the world via satellite from London as CNN bosses tested audience reaction to him. He was staggered and flattered by dozens of emails he received from relatives as well as colleagues, friends and fans, some of whom remembered Peter from his days at the BBC, ITN and long before, when his outing with fame first began as a mere child.

Peter, the third of ten children, was then always the joker of the family, performing in front of his parents and siblings, keeping everybody laughing. At prep and boarding schools, teachers found him to be other - worldly and mysterious in a charming sort of way. More importantly, Peter was also an excellent impersonator with a great speaking voice who could give stirring performances and he was inevitably chosen to take part in plays and inter-school debates. But he was also every bit the rapscallion, sometimes shirking his studies and blowing off school without exeat permission, to the eternal fury and disappointment of his parents, who like many Nigerian parents from educated backgrounds, were very disciplined and academically minded and insisted that all their children do extremely well.

At 16, having completed secondary school, Peter had a chance meeting with a famous Nigerian broadcaster who was impressed by Peter's diction and command of language. He arranged for an audition. Soon after, Peter was picked by the national broadcasting network as first an announcer, then six months later, a national network news presenter, giving him the distinction of being the youngest person to anchor Nigerian national news, up to that point.

25 years later, Peter had undergraduate and graduate degrees in broadcast journalism and television production from top American universities, a stint as a news director of a Cincinnati radio station, eight years experience as a broadcast journalist with Britain's main TV news networks and the polish and discipline of a seasoned professional.

CNN executives loved his cool unflappable style, clear diction and authoritative interviewing techniques, honed to near perfection as a news correspondent and presenter. *Flawlessly professional! Compulsively watchable! Unnaturally calm! Animate on cue! Striking resemblance to Trevor MacDonald, albeit a considerably younger version!* Peter was flushed with delight.

The deal had pretty much been concluded over the telephone and his trip to Atlanta was aimed at working out the fine print and meeting his new bosses. He had done it and there was more to come, Peter told himself smugly. This little boy was stepping forth!

Peter settled comfortably into his business class seat. He absent-mindedly flipped through newspapers handed to him by a horse faced Welsh flight attendant attempting one of those American TV toothpaste smiles presumably worn for the benefit of the many US passengers on board.

She was back minutes later bearing a tray laden with tuck: parcels of mixed vegetables wrapped in spinach, celery soup with bits of some kind of meat, prawn and lettuce in thousand-island dressing, roast breast of chicken on a veggie bed with sautéed potatoes. And as requested, one miniature bottle of Bordeaux Vin Rouge 1999 to go with the grub and a can of extra cold Guinness stout, his favourite tipple, to wash it all down afterwards. Peter attacked the food and drink hungrily.

When he had his fill, he retrieved the *Daily Mail* from a pouch in front of him. But he could only manage to get through the front page before he fell into a dreamless sleep.

Just after 5pm local Atlanta time, about 8 hours following takeoff, Peter, who had been kipping in staggered shifts of thirty odd minutes, roused with a start. Had he been snoring again? Had someone, an attendant perhaps, jolted him awake to shut him up?

The plane was banking sharply southward and Peter realised that a sudden drop in altitude had shaken him from his slumber. A few minutes later, with the rays of the setting sun gleaming off its skyline, he beheld a grand aerial view of Downtown Atlanta.

Half an hour passed and the plane touched down lightly. Peter gathered his belongings and joined the queue edging towards the exit, holding his passport and jacket in one hand and briefcase in the other.

Nothing warned him to be on guard. No cautionary notice informed him of impending danger. So, he was totally unprepared for what happened next.

1

Within seconds of stepping off the plane, Peter was surrounded by fierce looking United States Marshals, roughly pushed against the wall and handcuffed.

It happened so quickly. Peter had little time to react, save for his heart, which took instant fright. He let out a feeble low-pitched sound, a dull, flat, insipid emission expressing extreme fear.

The sound rasped out a question. "What the devil is going on?"

A beer-bloated plain-clothes Marshall with a large blunt-nose like a pit bull, dark hair and cold blue eyes addressed Peter. Such contempt in those hard eyes, his harsh cop voice coated with a thick, southern drawl, saying something that sounded terribly disjointed to Peter but which left him in no doubt that he was in a major pickle.

"We are US Marshals and you are on American territory…we have a warrant for your arrest from Hamilton County in Ohio for non-support of a dependent…you will be detained in Atlanta pending extradition to Cincinnati…stay calm and co-operate and this will be a lot easier for you".

Peter nodded wildly, uncomprehendingly. A large compound of incongruous, inhumanly misshapen elements, rather like animation characters, began to form and meander before his eyes. The beer-bloated Marshall became a giant bi-pedal pit bull. He read Peter his Miranda rights.

"You have a right to remain silent. Anything you say can and will be used against you…." And on he went.

When he finished, another powerfully built officer with a long trunk like the body of a lion rampant and a thin hawk-like face seized Peter's elbow with a large bony hand that felt like the claws of some swooping bird of prey, turning him around roughly -- one monster clutch, scraping Peter's skin, threatening to rip his arm clean off its socket with one mighty jerk if he didn't obey. One tugging twist followed by a sharp pull and it would be roughly but surely torn off. So Peter followed helplessly, stumbling along by the officer's side, the pit bull bringing up the rear.

People in economy class were still disembarking from the plane and now they were walking alongside Peter's motley party, clutching their trifles, witnessing his misfortune. Peter saw them gawking. A wave of humiliation washed over him. *Excited by my disgrace!* How they gobbled up this unexpected titillation. Out of the corner of his eye, he could make out a cameraman, in fact several camera operators, focusing on him. Alarm! Could that be the press? What were they doing *here* aiming their lenses at *him*?

Spasmodic contractions attacked Peter's muscles, forcing him to shake with fear. His heart, tachycardiac from the sudden exposure to danger, jolted and lurched, doing acrobatic somersaults at 105 beats. A sickening feeling of utter distress and fecklessness took hold of him. Into his mind's ear came a loud resonant metallic sound, the terrible clangour of the steel gates of a jail rattling shut behind him. Buried alive in a cold dark *American* mausoleum and forgotten! Trapped in a coffin with six feet of earth on top! Nothing but sepulchral, suffocating, howling panic!

Peter shrank from such fearful thoughts, which given their prolific fertility, was no easy task. He heaved and heaved, pushing them as far away from him as possible. Far far away, until they keeled over the edge and he pitched forward anxiously, head leaning over the rim, making sure the appalling things had properly lost their fecundity.

There had to be some mistake. His American lawyer had made arrangements with the prosecutor's office in Hamilton County and had assured him this was not going to happen. Peter feverishly ransacked his brain for an explanation, a way to rid himself of this mire. Maybe they thought he was someone else. Hadn't he read in *Readers Digest* that in America the law and its computers were always getting people mixed up? Perhaps as the article said some novice had cocked up. It was apparently not uncommon.

Peter tried to stay calm in his mind, but his body continued to convulse uncontrollably. A dreadful ringing began sounding in his head. Those fearful thoughts hadn't keeled over and died after all. Horrible! *Horrible!*

They entered a brightly-lit office. Peter's jaded eyes took in the grey walls and bolted down bench and heavy door. The airport police holding room. The Marshals proceeded to search his luggage. Peter had to speak.

"There's been a mistake", he said, trying to steady his voice... failing...his speech breaking up.   "I am not the person you are looking for".

The pit bull Marshal glared at him. Peter noticed large tufts of untrimmed hair growing thick on the ridge above his piercing eyes, like fetlocks on the back of a horse's hoof, giving him a distinctly satanic look.

"Liar", he snarled. "We were waiting for you and you're going to jail".

Did that ghastly hirsute Marshall just say *jail?* Anger overcame fear and clutched at Peter's core. His eyes flashed.

"Don't call me a liar", Peter barked, or thought he did, for in reality what the Marshals heard was a barely audible croak.

The pit bull Marshall, his blue eyes burning with hate, eyes that seemed to Peter would have pulverised him if they could, shoved him roughly against the wall. Southern red neck. Peter was utterly befuddled by the malevolence he saw in those eyes. Under their relentless assault, his mind staggered around in shock.

"Shut up", barked the pit bull Marshall. "I'm tired of listening to your bullshit".

Peter's alarm deepened dramatically. He felt desperation with a vengeance. Surely the mirthful value of this particular joke had been exhausted. It had gone the distance, as far as it could go.

Peter's voice moaned and pleaded, when what he wanted it to be was strong and masterful. But huge mothballs had somehow invaded the folds of the lining membrane of his larynx near the opening of the glottis. And now the edges were vibrating at half capacity, making him sound abnormally small and constricted, more like a whinnying horse alto than his usual growling tiger baritone.

"You don't understand. I have an important appointment with CNN in the morning and I've got to be there".

Peter refused to admit that this could be happening to him. Surely it was nothing more than an interesting but highly implausible yarn, a fairytale and this *pit bull* along with the rest of the monsters that had invaded his world were all imaginary characters out of one of his childhood books.

The pit bull cackled deep inside his windpipe. It sounded hoarsely resonant and deficient. His appearance transmogrified from a pit bull into the grotesque troll in *Three Billy Goats Gruff,* that famous Norwegian fairy tale.

"Forget it", he growled through a sucker mouth and vampire horny teeth. "That's one appointment you definitely ain't gonna keep".

Peter curled up inside, crushed. He saw the CNN job, something he had looked forward to more than anything else, fading away. His bridge to security and fame, gone in a slow flash dissolve. *A man without prospect! A person without importance!* He felt a tremendous presentiment of danger. Fear crashed over him like an angry wave. Nothing like this had ever happened to him before and it seemed certain worse was to come.

The troll Marshall came towards Peter and removed the cuffs. Then he barked in his thick, southern drawl.

"Okay, up against the wall, hands forward and spread your legs". *Laygs!*

Peter leaned forward awkwardly, hands against the wall, legs back. The troll Marshall kicked them apart from the inside, spreading him wide. His hands ran roughly, expertly up and down Peter's outstretched arms, collar, neck, shoulders, trunk, legs. Then the humiliation Peter feared most, as he felt Peter's testicles and penis and poked and prodded the crack of his arse.

Peter choked with incredulous shame. He tried to hold back the tears, catching his breath as they welled up, but they soon overflowed and he wept as silently as he could with gasping sobs. *Dear God,* he prayed fervently, *don't let this happen to me. Let me wake up in a minute.*

The troll Marshall pushed Peter through an inner door onto a bench in a dimly lit backroom. Then he leaned over, his face inches away …*blink! – loud sound of crashing! --* his crimsoned mug had reverted back to that of a monster pit bull. He grinned evilly. Then he was gone.

Hours passed. Peter fearfully contemplated his next move. He realised he had no choice but to stay put and wait. That was the hard part because he was so anxious. But he was also nearly out on his feet and he drifted exhaustedly in and out of fifteen-minute catnaps.

As evening turned to night, the pit bull Marshall returned accompanied by a lupine, rangy looking officer. *A werewolf walking on its hind legs lurks,* Peter thought deliriously. They twisted Peter's hands cruelly behind his back and fastened the handcuffs on tightly, raking his wrists as they did. *Lupus* placed a sinewy shaggy paw on Peter's shoulder and off they marched to the runway and into a waiting police vehicle.

Twenty minutes of racing through numbered streets, a manicured stretch of meadow, flashes of greenery, concrete and steel. Peter's wild frantic mind, taking it in! *Why if someone didn't nudge me right then I could have sworn I saw that green common there trying desperately, in a uniquely American way, to mask and hide the fact that this concrete jungle was just that, a concrete carbuncle. Strip it and you've got a junkyard. Nothing more, nothing less! As clearly as daylight he could see through their masked green-eyed hypocrisy...*

Peter's errant thoughts were interrupted as the patrol car skid stopped. They had arrived at their destination, the Clayton County jailhouse. Peter was hop hustled into admissions. His papers were handed over to the desk officer, a cross-eyed, overweight Latino with elephant ears and a waddling duck walk. A web-footed wading bird with bat ears and a lazy eye! He managed to fixate a scourging glare on both Peter and the computer screen in front of him. Peter felt as if one of those eyes was flogging him with long lash like feelers.

Presently webfoot signed a form and gave it to the delivering pit bull Marshall. Lupus his rangy colleague grinned sadistically at Peter then they were gone.

———

Peter looked around uneasily. Uniformed corrections officers and plain clothes police everywhere. Peter's breathing quickened, his heart thudded and galloped like herds of migrating wildebeest.

A fearsome American-bred Korean in uniform – face: broad flat yellow monolith...head: round and distended...ears: sticking out like ET -- came towards Peter menacingly. He gestured. Peter, drawing breaths in convulsive gasps, followed.

The Korean unlocked a steel door, removed Peter's handcuffs and pushed him in roughly. The doors crashed shut.

Peter was in a holding cell, a concrete windowless room equipped with a steel toilet and sink. The cell reeked of rotten food and stale urine. He shuffled over to a bolted down steel bench he saw directly in front of him, sitting uncomfortably, raging and brooding, stunned by his sudden loss of freedom.

Peter looked around nervously and noticed an inmate lying on the bare floor at the far end of the cell. He was stovetop black, in his twenties, unkempt, large, hairy and long limbed, like a giant hominoid. Peter's heart pounded as he regarded the great ape from the corner of his eye. Thankfully, he appeared to be fast asleep.

Peter lay down for a long time on the bench, staring at the ceiling, his mind blank, cell doors clanging loudly, shutting around him. *Crash*...irregular interval...another much louder *Crraasshh!!* Then another pause... an *interval of insanity*...then another jolting, earth juddering *Crrraaassshhh!!!*...Constant, back and forth!

Then imperceptibly, mental distress crept into his head, his mind, surreptitiously crawled down his spine, insinuated itself into his nervous system, gathered speed, making a crackling sound as it raced around his body. Various sententious expressions about the perverseness of things flowed through his mind. What kind of wicked treachery had his lawyer inflicted upon him? Peter had trusted him, paid him handsomely and he in turn had assured Peter everything was in order. Why didn't that bastard warn him this arrest was a possibility? Wasn't that his responsibility to his client?

Peter shivered with fatigue. He was stiff and sleepy and he felt an overwhelming sense of fear and despair. He was well and truly under the sod, in the grave. Help was clearly not on its way. He was not going to make it to CNN by morning.

He thought of his girlfriend Juliet back in London. She would be sleeping the sleep of utter guiltlessness, blissfully unaware of his plight. He longed to hold her close to him, but with each passing moment, the chance of that happening anytime soon seemed ever more remote.

He had no idea what was ahead of him, what horrors awaited him. It wasn't just the uncertainty of the outcome of what seemed likely to be a court case, but life over the next few days in *jail*, something with which he had no familiarity and which now loomed frightfully before him.

He closed his eyes. Suffocating aggressive paranoia. Demented fear of a future unknown gripping him by the throat and shaking him violently. Then a shadow appeared.

Peter half opened his eyes and his heart jumped. The hominoid was awake, a huge, disturbing spectre standing barely two feet away. Peter felt suddenly vulnerable lying on the bench, but he couldn't will himself to get up.

The hominoid moved closer. Through his eyelashes, Peter stole covert glimpses, more like photoflashes, of what looked like – what was that breed of dog – large strong breed with drooping ears and pendulous lips? ...Mastiff, that's it. *Flash!* Peter could see a mouth hanging half - open, tongue coiled like the elongated sucking organ in some worm. *Flash!* Ranks of gold teeth gleaming like a vault at the Bank of England. *Flash!* Tusk-like tubercles had somehow formed on the crown of his molar teeth, giving him a Mastodontic appearance. *Flash!* A two-legged, coarse, immensely powerful creature, *advancing*!

Peter tried to edge away on the narrow strip of bench and failed. Seen through Peter's eyelashes, the hominoid coming towards him seemed extremely sinister, like some kind of dire portent appearing just before Peter's death. An animal aura hung around the spectre. There was something disquietingly psychotic about the way he was staring at Peter, attempting to analyse him, struggling with what limited analytical faculties were available to him, sniffing Peter over like a search dog, irrational distrust blazing in his eyes.

He was now inches away. Peter knew because he could smell his breath. It was pungent and thick, reminding him of rotten eggs. Peter closed his eyes tightly lest the layer at the back of his eyeball that was sensitive to light -- the retina wasn't it -- forced his eye to open and behold that which was about to pulverise him.

Presently the hominoid grunted and Peter could hear him shuffling back to his corner. He must have thought Peter was asleep or else he was satisfied he did not pose a threat. Soon Peter could hear him snoring again.

Peter sat up and quietly walked over to the cell door, which was partly made of reinforced glass. He craned his neck trying to see if anyone was about. He looked down the far end of the long corridor.

He could see shoes approaching. Black and shiny, cracking against the concrete floor like a horsewhip! Peter's eyes followed the shoes, trailing up a body dressed in plain clothes till they encountered a clean-cut white face. Their eyes met. Peter's look of confusion and fear caught his attention. He paused.

"You're the guy with that accent from England they picked up at the airport, ain't you?"

"Yes", Peter replied, a wild look in his eyes.

He smiled. *Take counsel. I hear your cry.*

"Hard luck. Welcome to the most materialistic and unfair legal system in the western world, run by some of the most cruel, heartless and dumbest people on the planet". Peter's heart flew into tachycardia, racing at more than 105 beats per minute, as he muttered: "I need to get in touch with my fiancée in England and also the British embassy here. Can you help me and get me to a phone?"

Five minutes later the cell doors clanged open. The detective offered his hand. "The name is Chip. I've arranged for you to call England. I've also got you the phone numbers of the night desk at the British consulate here in Atlanta".

Peter gushed with gratitude. Hope *rekindled.*

The first person the operator connected Peter to was the man on the night desk at the British consulate in Atlanta. He appeared to have been taken quite by surprise. It was just after 11pm and he hadn't expected a call at that late hour in the night, much less a story as unlikely as Peter's. He seemed to have a kindly heart. He immediately saw how the matter stood.

"Good God, dear fellow", he muttered under his breath. "How utterly distressing. You may be assured sir that we'll take all necessary measures to assist you. Let's hope we hear the last of it soon". He undertook to ring friends and family around the world on Peter's behalf.

Then Peter got through to Juliet. His heart burst forth, releasing everything that had been pent-up inside him. She was horrified. Peter could hear her sobbing almost soundlessly. In his mind, he could see her big hazel eyes – eyelids curling upwards -- filling with tears, her lips and chin trembling, the tears beginning to flow down her cheeks.

But on the phone, down his ear, she tried to sound confident it would be over soon.

The operator cut in on the line to tell him time had expired. Peter felt as if barely a minute had gone by.

Later, Peter fell into a troubled sleep. The night was awful. He was cold and hungry and kept waking up from horrific nightmares. He dreamed he was in the Twilight Zone. He was stuck in a loop and didn't know how to get out of it.

By early morning, the bad dreams had given way to stonkered despair as Peter awoke and realised he would not make it to his appointment at CNN. Hope *extinguished*. *What do I do now that I've lost my job, my dream and my worth?*

Despair turned to fear and then horror of what he might have to do to survive in hell.

Twenty-four hours ago his life had been full of promise. Now it had become a puzzle from which several pieces had mysteriously vanished. *Walk away from it*, his heavy heart told him. *You simply can't go on. Have you thought of…I hate to say it…suicide?*

The cell door crashed open. Rude awakening in a filthy cell in Atlanta. Peter felt his heart beating far too fast as the morning ritual began with the serving of trays of disgusting food. Carton of milk. Stale bread. Congealed porridge.

Peter glanced at the clock in the hallway. 5.00am! He felt jumbled! His heart regularly skipped beats. He couldn't remember anything clearly. God, what was happening to him? Was this real, or was it some *existentialismus* game? Was he alive, or was he an instance of fictive creation, the product of the imaginative artistic intelligence of the chief prosecutor in Hamilton County, some piece of fiction contrived for the media? In that case, there was no escape.

He reached out, touching the tray hesitantly. Solid! He retracted his hand and let it rest on the bench he was sitting on. Also solid! He looked down at the thing that had extended from him and had just touched the objects. A hand! He wiggled the fingers. *His* hand! This was real. No question about it, he was done for.

Why hadn't this possibility occurred to him? Why had he come to America? Why had he trusted that traitorous lawyer? Why, why, why! He should have known. He should have bloody known! Judas conniver! Demanding several thousand dollars worth of silver!

He could have kept a simple radio job. Once a week on some obscure London radio station. But no! His colossal ambitions had brought him to this dead end and now he felt sick -- his scope, his world, visibly narrowing and unravelling before his eyes.

By 10a.m that morning, the promise of a CNN appointment had died. Instead, Peter was standing with his back to a wall. Several other new arrivals were lined up next to him. He was looking into the eyes of the angel of death. He was the jail equivalent of a drill sergeant, a huge dark muscular ursine beast with a thick moustache. His job was to crush any resistance and cut people down to size. He was like a god, full of power, brutal, invincible and intimidating.

He made a sudden menacing move forward...front leg bent at the knee...back leg straight - like an attack in fencing - driving the foul wind of unwashed bodies violently in Peter's direction, forcing Peter to take a couple startled steps backwards, till the wall breached further retreat.

When the angel of death barked, for that was what he did, his voice was sharp and thrusting, like a stab with a dagger. Peter almost turned and ran. But he knew that would be folly, so he swallowed hard and prayed.

Bark! Bark! Bark! Stab! Stab! Stab! Thrust! Thrust! Thrust! *I will degrade you! If you resist, you'll get beaten! If you get out of line, you'll get thrown in the hole! You are like an animal! The other Corrections Officers and me are your trainers. You will obey at all times. Strip butt-naked! I will strip search you. Then you take a shower! Then I will spray you with insecticide. All this time, you will remain butt-naked! I'll check you over, make you bend over and cough. Then you will get dressed in standard issue clothing. After that you will be taken to the sleeping cage or the slave camp. I call it that because when we say jump, you jump! If we say shovel shit, you shovel shit! We will read your letters and if we don't like it or you, we'll tear it up… You will be locked down for 23 hours a day…you will feel like you are an animal in a cage…but you are not allowed to go insane…after ten days those who are to be extradited will be shipped out…*

Oh God! Oh God! Oh God! Was this America or somewhere else, some totalitarian state in the old Eastern Europe or Asia, Nigeria under the dictatorial grip of General Abacha? What unspeakably monstrous thing had he, Peter, done to the gods to earn their wrath?

———

Peter was only just beginning to learn the horrors of the American penal system. He was locked up in the same cage as murderers, thieves and rapists. At first he thought it was a mistake, but he soon learned that because he was a foreigner, he was considered to be a flight risk. So he was dressed in maximum security red and caged with the most violent offenders, the most unsavoury characters. All around the large dormitory cell, men -- boys mostly, really -- in various states of despair, in the prime of their youth, severed from normality by an unforgiving system. Functional illiterates, debased by society. Angry street dogs, snapping and howling and raging and frothing at anything and everything.

Peter's corner mate was one of the more pleasant chaps. In his late thirties with a Hispanic mocca complexion, he had been caught with several kilos of cocaine and an AK47 assault rifle. He had a prior conviction for murder -- shot his cousin nine times and served ten years. He whispered conspiratorially to Peter that he had killed at least two others but was never caught. He admitted he had taken part in several armed robberies and had no feelings of remorse.

A few feet across from Peter the chocolate coloured serial killer had his beddings. Thin, tall and bearded, in his early forties, with a string of robberies and murders, including children, across several states. Made a pact with his white wife to both blow their brains out if they were ever caught. Cornered in Atlanta, she killed herself, but he chickened out.

Down beyond the smelly lavatory, the 17-year old, in for three murders and cutting a dog to pieces. The reckoning is he'll get the chair. But he's not buying it.

"Them mo'fuckers wan' fry my black ass, but I aint gon' let them. I got me ten years of appeals and I'm gon' win".

Next to him, the white child molester, beaten severely and allegedly raped by inmates...

Oh God! Oh God! Oh God! Peter felt as if he was living in a sea of human rubbish. To him the place looked like a galactic zoo. *What planet are you from mate?* He drifted in and out of sleep, half opening his eyes, seeing various half people walking around -- limbs, waists, shoes. Back to front! Front to back!

Hours pass. His vision blurs. A half man with a dark snake hanging from his face walks shiftily by. His vision clears. A naked black man.

Hours pass. *He wants to run out where the day meets the night, far beyond these mid west farms,* says the commercial on television. How true!

The loudspeaker suddenly crackles into life.

"England, you have a message from your sister Priscilla in California".

Relief flooding through him. The man at the British Consulate had kept his word. Peter was no longer alone.

More messages of hope, from his relatives in London, Ireland and Nigeria. *Do not be afraid. It's God and us and who needs anyone else?*

Days pass.   Villainous characters prowl the corridors -- up and down, down and up -- hurling curses, constantly displaying, rich in violent suggestion, wild animals in a large cage, minds seriously screwed up by society -- one wasn't sure how badly, which made them appear even more frightening and dangerous to Peter.

Then, finally Peter is able to speak with the lawyer in Cincinnati that he hired from London. A sense of unease pervaded the conversation. Peter remembered Shakespeare's line. *First thing we do, let's kill all the lawyers!* He made a mental note to develop a greater admiration for Shakespeare at some future date when life was less stressed. Then he remembered with a flash of regret that his father, his eldest brother and a number of relatives were all lawyers.

"Why didn't you tell me?" Peter shouted at him down the phone.

"I told you these people are devils", he replied with irritating quiet.

"That's not good enough", Peter yelled. "You assured me. You must have known indictments generally aren't worked out. You're supposed to be a bloody barrister for chrissake".

"I can't do anything for you right now until you get down to Hamilton County. Then we'll try and get you out".

Did that creep say *try?* Peter was bewildered and angry. He wanted to punch the man's face.

"How am I to survive in here while you try?"

The lawyer's response carried little conviction. He told Peter how sorry he was about everything, but after he hung up, Peter felt depressed. He could tell the man wasn't the least bit remorseful.

2

—————

DAY FIVE IN CLAYTON County jail. Peter lay on his beddings staring into space. It was just after lunch and inmates had returned to their corners for a compulsory period of "quiet time". The muffled, deep sound of a heavy flatus tightly expelled through an anus – it could be any one of several in the immediate vicinity -- rolled towards Peter's corner like the rumble of low-level thunder, followed slowly by a noxious, putrescent stench that seemed to grow bigger and more rotten by the second. Like the smell of those night soil men, their bucket latrines oozing effluvium, along *Obiagu* road in *Enugu*, one of the places Peter recalled in southeastern Nigeria still without flush toilets and sewage systems. The fetid fumes hung in the air, like a scene from the Road – Runner, *Wily Coyote* suspended in mid air before the inevitable fall. Then the evil funk paraded past Peter into the hallway, trailing gagging sounds and angry responses in its wake, finally losing its odorous self outside the cage, somewhere in that maze of corridors.

Shouting from criminal yonder over there! A skinny young man had made the mistake of accusing a *gang-banger* of blowing the wind that stank up the room. In effect, he had pointed a finger at all six members of the same gang who were seated together watching a re-run of *The Jeffersons*.

They pounced with feral, infuriated barbarity. He screamed, struggling to fight them off. They kicked and punched him, six against one. His arms and legs were in the air. They looked as if they were going to be wrenched from his body, torn limb from limb.

Suddenly, Peter felt someone frantically tugging at his arm. It was his corner mate.

"Quick, git your black ass over to the far side, brother. If the guards come, they gon' be spraying every body nearby with pepper spray".

In spite of the noise, the guards, who were no doubt watching through the monitors in their tower, never appeared. It was rumoured that he pissed them off and so now they were letting him get a right clobbering as a warning to other inmates.

From a safer coign of vantage and with his heart banging in his chest like steel drummers at London's Notting Hill Carnival, Peter watched the ferocious savaging. One of the brutes threw a sheet over the victim, blinding and confusing him. Blows and kicks rained down on him. He stumbled pitifully, threw a haphazard, ill-aimed punch, collided with a fist, walked into a well-aimed kick, tripped and bounced to the ground. Splotches of bright red appeared on the white sheet. Another vicious kick to the stomach! Peter could hear the air whooshing out of him. He struggled to his feet, lurched and lunged wildly but was quickly brought down again. The hammering of the blind! No one intervened.

Then suddenly, it stopped. The animals had temporarily slaked their blood lust. Peter could hardly breathe from fear. The victim, doubled over, was moaning and trying to catch his breath. He managed to extricate himself from the sheet. His face was swollen and severely bruised. A mixture of blood and saliva dribbled from his half-open mouth. Splinters of teeth, some of them shimmering with gold, were embedded in his lower lip. He tottered drunkenly for a moment. Then he collapsed.

Peter's corner mate was rooted to the spot, his eyes wide, breathing heavily, his face lit up with excitement.

"Man! That was some ass whuppin'! Sweet Judas!"

Peter's head whirled. He prayed silently but fervently. *I can't believe the things I see. I have slipped into a fourth world of insanity. I have taken up residence in Subterrania! There is no way I can manage another second of this. If they can do that to this poor chap, then there is no escape. Sooner or later, something horribly untoward is bound to befall me. Lord I pray. Give me strength to carry on!*

Minutes passed. Inmates on outside detail came in and removed the victim. He was semi-conscious. That was the last Peter saw of him.

Day 6! Peter refused to confirm the grim reality of the place. As often as he could, he shut his eyes to the world of despair around him. *There will be no waking nightmares for me. Let the horrors come to me in my sleep.*

And they did! His eyes tightly closed, he imagined he saw mischievously energetic beings from the world of the damned malignantly coiling concentric circles around his soul, threatening to strangle his spirit. Eventually, his resolve faltered. He woke up tired, forced to open his eyes. His corner mate said he understands.

"It's hard to sleep when you can't be sure the guy you pissed off during the day ain't gonna piss on you while you sleep".

Peter lay there wondering how he was going to fill this day that seemed to stretch endlessly in front of him. This day that demanded endurance, cunning and extraordinary strength to pull through in such harsh circumstances, a battle to survive not just oneself but each other, trying to keep one step ahead of the game. He was so different from what they were used to. Most couldn't tell where the rest of the world outside their own city fitted in on a world map. They had spent their lives in borstals -- reform schools whose therapies had failed to remove the delinquency inside. Instead of maths and English, they had been schooled in criminal practices from an early age. They didn't have chips, they had logs on their shoulders. Frightfully volatile maniacs, who at any moment, on the slightest provocation, a mere suggestion, could snap and become agitated and violent. It could be as simple as a sideways glance construed by a drug-crazed mind to be threatening.

For Peter, it was a scary experience in survival. He tried to put as much distance between they and he as possible. He never got to know most of the characters. Never even exchanged a word. They were like ghosts, cut off from life, shadows of the living, abstract forms that never crystallised into reality in his subjective world. From time to time a face would appear fleetingly and he would wonder: who was he, what was he? And then just as quickly it would vanish into a distant place.

Mid morning! Sleep, Peter's only comfort, veiled his eyes. *I can see you Jul, entering my dreams like a spirit, lying on the bed next to me, in a world far from here. Your skin tanned to bronze by years under a relentless Australian sun. Your long curls piled high on top of your gorgeously shaped head. Tall lithe and slender with full lips, pert breasts and a figure that could start a stampede. No one could be more beguiling. I reach out to hold you. You turn towards me slowly, shivering. You purr contentedly. I smile. I am happier than I have ever been. "Hello friend", I whisper. Then suddenly, your beatific face starts to swim away from me. I reach out with an awkward hand but instead of pulling you closer, I push you further and further away until you disappear.*

Peter woke up into desolation and fear and emptiness. He was barely alive in his grave. He wished he had a drink, even a joint. Surely after all this, he deserved something to set him free for a while, to let him float away from there.

Daydreams and involuntary visions, passing through his mind. Images, thoughts, emotions. *To little Chinny, the daughter I never saw. For all the days I never spent with you, for all the things you have become without me. Is it true that every parent is blessed with the right child? That the life we are living is the one we are meant to have? That we all grow up feeling emotionally distant from at least one parent?*

The image of her little face floated up to Peter.

I remember you all those years ago, during my one visit to you. Sitting on the small stool in your room, watching you assembling your toys. Your enthusiasm for them is evident, but you chat to me hesitantly at first, looking me hard in the eyes. I smile and wink, but feel fear and guilt. I see pain in your eyes. I wonder what you see in my face. Betrayal? I watch entranced as you quietly but firmly eliminate all pyjama suits on offer, insisting on a nightgown. A lady already! Then you fall asleep. How have I damaged you?

By late afternoon, Peter was feeling slightly more alive. Detective Chip -- bless him -- gave Peter the rare opportunity of ringing London again and speaking with Juliet. He had also given Peter a copy of *USA Today*. Peter was reading about Mehmet Ali Agca, the man who shot Pope John Paul the second on May 13, 1981. (Ironically, Peter himself had met the Pope in 1999). The Pope had apparently disclosed that Agca's attack was predicted beforehand in a message given by a spectral appearance of the Virgin Mary to the three children of Fatima in 1917 in Portugal. It was the third and last "Secret Of Fatima" revealed by the Pope during a visit to the shrine early in 2000.

Fascinating thought Peter. Was his own arrest, detention and humiliation, simply "part of a cameo role in the mysterious project of God", as Agca put it? Was this part of God's plan, a piece of a jigsaw that was pre-destined? Was he, Peter, "destiny's tool?"

Peter waited for seven days to be extradited. Though it was a relatively short period of confinement, nevertheless it had begun to take its toll, gradually but steadily enfeebling his mind. Peter recalled some jail-house writer who described what was happening to him thus: *First there is fear, then discontent followed by panic attacks and loss of appetite as spirits begin to break. After this, most people spend many hours sitting in the same position, staring lugubriously into space. The prolonged inactivity in jail makes things worse. People lose their sense of time and wellbeing and fall into protracted silences. This is the last stage before deep suicidal depression sets in. Some people never recover from this stage and a few are placed on suicide watch.*

Peter never degenerated to the suicidal fringe. But he did become delirious. He followed the hands of the clock on the wall as it ticked along. He watched the hour hand then the minute hand then the second hand, willing them to move faster. They did the opposite. Then to his troubled mind they stopped moving altogether. The days conspired with the clock and also stopped moving. Shadows would not shorten or lengthen. Perspectives remained fixed. Everything under that hideous fluorescent light became static. Day in, day in, day in, but no day out.

Peter floated in and out of sleep, like a drunken man. Dodgy characters meandered in and out of the shadows. The air was cold and stiff. No need to wash or change because there was no way out. Life had become a bad dream. He could not find words nor will. He could not eat or read. He felt himself depreciating rapidly, becoming of little worth, like a sudden decline in the purchasing value of a convertible paper currency. He was deeply scared. Would he ever find himself again?

He became suspicious of his bed sheets, his pillow and his mattress. They were in on it, part of the massive conspiracy against him. He had to find a way to control them, master them. Henceforth, he would place the pillow, no *lock* the pillow, in his locker. No more whispering bitter conspiracies to the mattress.

Somehow, he trusted the blanket but nothing else. He began to feel pleased with his plan. Then he woke up with a start.

FLASHBACK

Peter's story began from a point in time and space thirty-nine years ago, the moment when he was born in Glasgow Scotland, the third of ten children. His Nigerian father had been Cambridge and Bristol trained as a lawyer and it was his desire that his third son be born in the UK. So he sent Peter's pregnant Mom to Cambridge Technical College for further studies and while she was holidaying in Scotland, Peter was born.

The next decade was spent with a blur of nannies whose names Peter barely remembered, but whose bodies he and his elder brothers had grown up lusting over and never forgot; in multi-racial private "crammer" schools, which Peter hated because to his mind at the time they were basically created for no other reason than to make pupils like himself, who horrified their parents by inclining to idleness, work bloody hard; and a three-year civil war in Nigeria during which Peter witnessed inflictions of extreme anguish.

It was during the war that Peter became sexually aware. He remembered well the events that marked his discovery of carnal pleasures. He had just turned nine and his imagination was vivid with lustful imagery, sharpened by a series of practical lessons given to Peter and his mates by a nineteen year old teenager, Domingo, on the delicate art of sexual gratification through self-stimulation, otherwise known in vulgar slang as "wanking". Domingo, who was given to the appetites and passions of the body, filled their young heads with stories about sensual indulgence and how to seduce women, including and rather dangerously Peter now thought on reflection, other people's women.

A couple of days later, like a self-fulfilling prophecy, Domingo had been caught in the act, working the girlfriend of that brutal Second Lieutenant with the protruding jawline and six pack abs, known only by his nickname *Uwa Nkaa Sef*, meaning "this world of ours" -- an expression he used so often that it stuck -- and by reputation as someone who enjoyed inflicting severe pain in an effort to twist or force confessions out of the enemy. *Uwa Nkaa* (the name had always sounded to Peter like a corruption of *"wanker"* or *"you wanker"*) had returned early from one such assignment at headquarters – apparently the victim had died suddenly under torture. Still adrenaline charged, *Uwa Nkaa* had come silently upon Domingo while the latter was in the formers' single-bedroom flat deep-throating his girl. Then as Domingo eased himself out and prepared to blast her with his arousal, *Uwa Nkaa* raised his baton and brought it down with unbelievable force on Domingo's protruding backside, causing him to yell out in pain and surprise and at the same time spray gobs of semen and saliva all over both *Uwa Nkaa* and the girl. Which of course further infuriated the soldier, so that he charged Domingo with his baton, raining blows on him. And it was only when he paused to pull out and cock his service revolver that a stark naked Domingo, suffering from a broken wrist and numerous other injuries, managed to tumble down the stairs and out of the building. And for the rest of the war, Domingo walked with a limp and earned himself the nickname *"Tarsip"*, mimicking the noise made by a dripping water tap and supposedly his cum spraying penis as he fled *Uwa Nkaa's* wrath.

The girl was never seen or heard from again. But the image of her spread apart by Domingo became the trigger that started Peter's active sexual life. It created a pathway to lust in his brain, which would light up with testosterone and force him to whack it whenever he recalled the picture.

––––

Fast-forward thirty years. The image of Peter's adversary, the *woman*, portrayed by the prosecutor as a paragon of womanhood -- *innocent, wronged, cast out* and *abandoned* – had risen up before his eyes. He held it there for a moment. The face was indistinct but the body Peter remembered well, despite the intervening years. The voluptuous suggestion of her loamy parted thighs, tongue sticking out treacherously like the serpent, inviting him in, seducing him into the same *Venus lips* his brother once knew, except in Peter's case it had turned into *Venus flytrap*.

Peter had met the *woman* in 1980, two days after he arrived in the United States to pursue a Bachelor of Science degree at Xavier University in Cincinnati. His elder brother, Zik, with whom she was already having a sexual relationship – yes, that's true! - made the proxy introduction. He had just graduated from Xavier and was on his way out. He asked her to "help Peter find his feet in… an alien environment". He later said he had explicitly appealed to her not to get involved with Peter sexually, because knowing her the way he did, he suspected she would.

Not that he cared particularly. At the time he had numerous girlfriends most of whom he did not really take seriously.

Peter was barely at the end of his teens. *The woman* was about seven years older than he and five years ahead of his brother Zik. She became a sort of tour guide for Peter around Cincinnati.

One night, after about one week of shopping and sight seeing, she invited Peter over to her house on Paddock road about twenty minutes drive from Brockman Hall, his campus dormitory. She was a great cook and dinner was impeccable: peppered American super size jumbo prawns for starters. Then stewed beef with fried plantains and fresh salad with a homemade dressing. Chilean red wine that made Peter more than a little light-headed.

After dinner, she complained about how unseasonably hot it was. Almost carelessly and apparently without great thought, she casually slipped the oversize warmer top she was wearing over her head. Then still acting unconcerned, she unbuttoned her jeans and unmethodically rolled them down her hips to her feet. She was naked except for a sleeveless, plunging under shirt that barely contained her ample breasts, stopping just above her belly button.

Peter caught sight of her nakedness. The effect was immediate. Seeing her standing there, virtually starkers, her plump thighs, her oddly flattened bottom and everything else in full view, he felt himself go rigid as *Omar*. The sight took hold of his young mind, remorselessly turning it crazy with her sex.

With a dazed expression, Peter's eyes followed her every move. She clasped and unclasped her hands over her breasts and privates, in some false attempt at womanly modesty, all the while eyeing him with an amused look, taking in the effect of her nakedness on his youth.

A small voice inside Peter's head warned him to leave the *femme fatale* alone. He ignored it. She came towards him, her breathing quick and uneven, lubricious lust in her round eyes. Peter felt a tumescent surge of reckless desire. The woman was a voluptuary. The prurience he detected in her eyes made him want to lock her in passionate enjoyment right there on the kitchen floor. Such lewd sensuous suggestion oozing from her, filling him with a richly sweet sensation of hot arousal! Pausing only for the briefest of kisses, she led Peter into her bedroom and hurriedly undressed him. When he touched her, she responded like she was demented. The flytrap opened wide, flashing its bait, swelling him bigger. He plunged in quickly, deeply, helping himself enthusiastically.

When it was over, desire speedily turned to aversion. Peter was startled by how quickly he had succumbed to her seductive charm. All he wanted to do was flee. He felt as if he had been taken over by a powerful spirit.

The fact remains that you woman were much older than he, in fact older than me as well and had the advantage of familiarity with the environment into which he necessarily had to find his feet, Peter's brother Zik, wrote in a letter to her much later, after the shit had hit the fan. *You were therefore in a much better position to have steered the relationship towards a different modus operandi. Instead you succumbed to your own desires and to some extent took advantage of his dependence on your friendship and youthfulness in the new environment…*

After that first encounter and a couple more, both *the woman* and Peter agreed the relationship would amount to no more than pure physicality given the age gap and her previous relationship with his brother Zik. During the next few years, they went their separate ways, dating other people, meeting and sleeping together once or twice in between relationships. She was a sexy woman, hard to resist when there was nothing going. Peter just couldn't see that she was leading him on, as his brother Zik put it, *an older woman concerned with the ticking of her biological clock, with no male partner in sight, making the unilateral decision to become pregnant.*

In fact, said Zik, *I would have been the one that might have fallen into that "trap". If your memory serves you well, you will remember once towards the tail end of my stay in Cincinnati when you suspected that you had become pregnant. You were very indignant about having the baby, despite my equally forceful protest that I was neither ready to shoulder the burdens of fatherhood nor interested in marrying you. We ended up going to see a doctor who thankfully confirmed that contrary to your suspicions, you were not pregnant, but merely had a delayed menstrual cycle...*

In 1986, after a short visit to England and Nigeria, Peter returned to America and prepared to move to Columbus, Ohio, to begin a Masters degree programme at the Ohio State University. *The woman* suddenly began telephoning him again. Peter had not seen or heard from her in three years.

A four-year relationship with his girlfriend at the time, a fashion model from the US Virgin Islands who had been crowned Miss *Black* Cincinnati, had just ended. Whilst with her, Peter had been infatuated with another female. The whole sordid mess finally exploded in his face.

And so a month after they parted ways, Peter was birdless, unhappy and vulnerable once again not only to the *woman's* seductive charm, but also to his own need for emotional and sexual healing.

Following the split, Peter had become rampant, oscillating between casual relationships and one-night stands. So it didn't take much convincing for him to respond to a female like the *woman* whose sexuality was coming through thick as treacle down the phone.

You need a shoulder to cry on, she purred, inviting him to her house for a "special dinner".

Come the day, Peter remembered being a little puzzled that she seemed uncharacteristically tense and stiff.

Anything on your mind, love? He asked.

On my mind baby? Of course not! I was just worrying about you… forget your troubles…Come into my island…I'll play you a song to fill the hours till morning…how about Jon Lucien or Roberta Flack? I need some reassurance too…have another drink…forget about the clock on the wall that says it's time to leave…Let me blow on your glass so you'll know you're still alive…forget the raincoat…didn't you know? Complications of the womb mean I cannot bring forth your seed…just ask the doctor…or your brother…

After dinner, she went into the living room, lay down by the fireplace, swung up her legs and crooked a finger at him. The casual gesture turned Peter's mind upside down. He silently called on the Almighty to help him resist this delicious temptation. But the Almighty was clearly engaged elsewhere. So he spread her legs and pounded her hard right there on the floor, making her scream with pleasure.

Peter neither saw nor heard from her again for the next three months. Meanwhile, he moved to Columbus to begin a Masters degree programme at The Ohio State University. He also started dating a gorgeous journalism student from Puerto Rico.

Then one day, out of the blue, the *woman* telephones. Her words are etched in bold strokes on Peter's mind forever:

I'm pregnant, you are the father and I'm definitely having the baby.

Peter felt a sudden and disturbing physical reaction like a violent collision, a massed cavalry charge, an acute state of prostration, impact tremor, pathological shock. Horror! Outrage! Fear! Disgust!

Dark doubt immediately came upon him. How could she be sure it was his?

She insisted there could be no mistake.

He felt numb! He realised the whole thing had been pre-meditated – a trap. She knowingly invited him over while she was ovulating. He remembered how she had insisted on choosing the date and the time of their last meeting.

Didn't you tell me you couldn't have children?

Well, I was obviously mistaken, came the answer.

You lied to me.

No reply!

He tried to reason with her.

"Look, I am a foreign student and I simply do not have the financial capability to raise a child. Besides I do not believe in having children out of wedlock, I am certainly not going to marry you and I'm definitely not ready for the burdens of fatherhood".

No response! Extra cold silence!

Peter saw his ambitions for global conquest disappearing under the yoke of dirty diapers. Desperate, he told her that as a non-American, there was no chance of him remaining in the United States and this would be unfair to the child.

"I don't intend to make any demands of you", she said calmly. "I am a successful psychologist and I can afford to raise my child myself".

And so, Peter's brother Zik said, *you made the fateful decision that if in the course of your sexual liaisons with myself and subsequently my brother you were to get pregnant, you would carry the pregnancy to term. You found ample and convenient justification for that self-serving position of yours in religious dogma and doctrine. Yet, the same religious dogma and doctrine which you invoked to justify the end which you sought, failed to deter you from indulging your sexual desires in the first place...*

Peter felt weak! One night of passion and now this. He wanted so much to yell at her. *Vile temptress! How I despise thee!* But he bit his tongue savagely and somehow kept his cool.

In January 1987, the *woman* gave birth to a pretty baby girl. Peter went to see her. The *woman* glowed with pride, her voice triumphant, her words never to be forgotten. *I accept all the responsibility for what happened. I urge you to get on with your life. In fact I insist that you live your life unencumbered by parenthood towards this child.*

Six months later, Peter graduated from Columbus and moved to London, England.

He telephoned her from London shortly after he arrived, but her number had lapsed. He found out later that she had moved to Florida and got married to some guy whom she described as "the man I love".

In the interim, Peter himself got married and had a delightful baby daughter. He also became a news correspondent with the BBC. He was heard and seen on radio and television across the world.

The woman was one of many who listened with rapt attention to rebroadcasts of Peter's BBC reports on the American National Public Radio network – everything from coverage of the collapse of the former Soviet Union and the crisis that engulfed Nigeria following the annulment of presidential elections in June 1993 to neo-Nazi activity in Austria and much more. She was greatly impressed and immediately re-established contact, urging Peter to come through Cincinnati, where she had made home once again.

Peter went to see her during one of his visits to America and discovered that her marriage attempt had failed. She began to look the part of the artful plotter when she announced that she had written to Peter's parents to inform them about "their grandchild", something she had failed to do for several years. She appeared quite taken by his regular appearances on radio and television, something most Americans associate with big earnings. Nothing of course could be further from the truth. How could he impress upon her that he was earning British wages: no more than 28,000 pounds sterling annually, the equivalent of about

46,000 American dollars in terms of buying power.   But if she heard, she did not take any notice.

Peter's suspicions deepened when a letter from a government affiliated medical institution in Cincinnati arrived at the BBC asking him to submit to a voluntary paternity test to determine "once and for all, the doubtful paternity of an Ohio citizen…". Peter agreed and six weeks later, it came back positive.

As a consequence, Peter wrote to the *woman* and requested a breakdown of the child's monthly expenses as well as her earnings so he could contribute his share. She responded that she intended to let the courts decide. Peter's brother Zik subsequently wrote to her also offering to make payments towards the child's upkeep on behalf of Peter. No response!

Barely a month later, in the autumn of 1996, the *woman* went before a magistrate in Hamilton County. Reading a transcript of the proceedings, Peter could not believe such bold-faced lying under oath.

Q: *How long did you have a relationship with the defendant, first of all?*

A. *We met in 1981. My daughter was conceived in '86. And we dated from 81 to 86 (lie number 1).*

Q: *And do you have knowledge of the defendant's employment history?*

A: *Yes I do. He's an assistant bureau chief with the BBC (lie number 2).*

Q: *All right. And what knowledge do you have of his income?*

A: *When he was here two years ago, he offered $700 a month, which was very little to him (lie number 3). He said he had just hired a full time, live-in nanny to avoid the boring 3:00 feedings for Amanda (who???) (lie number 4). And I am also aware that the reason he had not paid earlier was that his houses had gone vacant for three months and that put a sting in his income (lie number*

5).   He has never until now denied paternity. We have been in contact all these years…this wasn't some fly by night romance. He was in love…(lie number 6).

Q: Okay what I need to hear is bottom line dollars. Do you know how much -- if he says he earns what turns out to be $49,000 a year in US dollars --

A: He has -- he earns at least twice that much (lie number 7)…When he was here three years ago he showed me the labels -- he showed up in Armani, had no compunction about it (lie number 8)…he had no compunction about telling me that for her birthday, he bought his wife a flat in Paris because they were under such stress (lie number 9). I know that he has purchased buildings since he left in '82…(lie number 10)

Q: All right. I am going to use a hundred thousand dollars for him… I am going to make it effective from date of birth…that's $878 a month plus an extra $100 per month in arrearage…

And that was that. In a hot second, by perverse order of a magistrate and a monumental travesty of justice, Peter was suddenly owing the *woman* more than $100,000 in child support payments back dated to the birth date of 1987 when he was a struggling graduate student with no earnings to speak of. Plus he now had to find an extra $1000 a month roughly to send to her in America. It was such a preposterous charade.

Peter needed legal advice. The Citizens Advice Bureau in north London informed him that Britain did not have an extradition agreement with the United States over child support cases and that if Peter decided to simply ignore the court order, they would not have a chance in hell of getting a penny from him. However the advise from the CAB chap was to "file an objection. Let them know you are eager to contribute as you should, although certainly not the astronomical amount imposed so unfairly by the magistrate". This was the course of action Peter chose.

At the time of course, he had no idea he was facing criminal charges that could land him in what can only be described as debtors jail and leave him with a possible felony record if found guilty. He assumed it was a civil case, which is what prevails in Britain.

In November 1996, Peter filed an objection through the Prosecutors office at the Hamilton County Juvenile Court in Cincinnati. He asked the court to set aside the decision which he believed to be outrageous and absurd, but most of all, largely unfair. He pointed out that the magistrate had not taken into account the reality of his pre-tax salary or the fact that he had another dependent child. The court had also ignored the background to the case showing clearly that *the woman* had made a unilateral decision to have the baby. She had rejected all previous offers of a reasonable payment and had allowed an intervening period of nine years to elapse before filing any claims in court. And of course that her claims about Peter owning properties all over Europe and earning in excess of 100,000 dollars a year were totally false. Nor did they "date" for any period of time.

Peter never received a response from the court. Many months later, he did hear from them indirectly and in a rather very crude manner. By this time he had been through a divorce and had gone into freelance work, having volunteered to leave the BBC after nearly eight years and seek a fresh environment. (The BBC under John Birt had approved a round of voluntary and compulsory redundancies and a general purge of permanent staff positions was underway. Peter opted for voluntary redundancy). After a year as a general reporter for the British independent television network, ITN and a couple of months in limbo, Peter had been reincarnated on a short-term contract as Chief Press Officer for the *Drop the Debt* Campaign. It was a formidable coalition of international stars and organisations dedicated to focusing attention on the burden of third world debt. Peter began working closely (but for very little money) with such well known campaigners as Sir Bob Geldof, U2's Bono, Quincy Jones, Randall Robinson, Jesse Jackson, Payne Lucas, the Dalai Lama, Nelson Mandela and

President Obasanjo of Nigeria, as well as The Vatican, Lambeth Palace (the Archbishop of Canterbury) and the American Treasury Secretary, Larry Summers.

Peter was organising a huge public relations meeting between the Pope and numerous pop stars to focus attention on the unpayable debt of the world's poorest countries, when a fax came through to his desk from his brother Zik in Columbus -- the one who had introduced him to *the woman*.

It was a copy of a newspaper article with the bold caption: "69 Indicted for Non Support".

Next to the headline was a photo of Peter's face with the words: "worst offender".

His heart galloping, Peter excused himself from his desk and went to the privacy of the lavatory where he read the rest of the article in stunned silence.

If they weren't all on Ham County's list of "deadbeat parents" they would have almost nothing in common. One is a former Bengals running back who earned more than $500,000 a season before moving to Great Britain. Others include a truck driver from Arizona, a corporate executive and an international radio correspondent last seen in West Africa. All were named Thursday in what prosecutors described as the largest mass indictment in county history. Prosecutors say the 65 men and four women owe a total of nearly $1.3 million to 107 children. "These are the worst of the worst," said Prosecutor Mike Allen. "They have violated the non-support statute as badly as it can be violated".

Peter's hands started shaking very badly. He could hardly believe what he was reading. He skimmed through the article until he saw his name again.

Mr Allen said the worst offender is (Peter Oti), a former correspondent for the British Broadcasting Corporation who owes about $135,000. (Mr Oti), who most recently worked in West Africa, is accused of failing to support his 12-year old daughter for more than a decade. The daughter and her mother recently moved from Ham County to Chicago...

His picture in the newspaper, with that caption, those head-lines! *Worst Offender!* Unbelievable! The horror, engulfing his entire being. *Got to pull myself together. Thrash this thing out. My picture...worst offender...Ham County's most wanted...*

Peter's hands shaking, he rang up the newspaper in Cincinnati and spoke at length to the reporter who had written the story. Peter gave him as much background as he could remember and the reporter promised to do another version. He never did.

Next Peter phoned the Hamilton County prosecutors office.

"I'm sure we can work something out", the man lisped slyly, "but you need to hire a lawyer in Ham and come down here to attend Juvenile Court".

Shortly after, Peter's contract with the *Drop the Debt* Campaign ended. There was much more on offer elsewhere and Peter chose not to renew it. CNN International put him on air as a casual news anchor. At the same time, Peter hired the lawyer who led his hands to the chains of incarceration. Peter told him that he was prepared to appear before the Juvenile Court in Cincinnati because he was convinced they didn't have a case against him. Soon after, CNN invited Peter to Atlanta to formalise a perma-nent contract as a news anchor.

Peter immediately made plans to go to Atlanta from where he intended to travel to Hamilton County. The lawyer left a mes-sage saying he had spoken with the prosecutor's office and there would be no problem as long as Peter stuck with the agreement to come to Cincinnati voluntarily. They never gave him the chance to keep his word.

Peter Oti, *fugitive from US law*, was arrested as he set foot on American soil. So now he lived in a world of constant flux.

PART TWO

---

*(In Flamman Moriendum Est: Into
The Flame For We Must Die)*

EXTRADITION

THURSDAY, 18TH. PETER'S HANDS and feet and waist were shackled for his extradition from Atlanta in the southern United States to Hamilton County in the state of Ohio – the bridge to the mid west. His shoelaces have been removed in case he is suicidal. The van arrived at 7am and Peter was hustled in. He was chained to a mixed race guy who was already in the mini bus. He shot and killed someone and was facing a possible death sentence. He was twenty.

The two officers, male and female extradition agents, were methodical, bored even. The male officer told Peter that he had been doing the job for over twenty years.

"So don't fuck with me, England, or I'll fuck you up". The female agent chain-smoked, took polaroid pictures of Peter from different angles and said very little.

They began their journey, which would take the whole day and most of the next. They headed first to county jails across the state of Georgia to pick up other inmates. The wretched of the earth! One was a white guy facing ten years in prison for manufacturing ecstasy and life or death for murder. Another, an African American *dread* charged with armed robbery was so smelly, Peter had to draw breath in snatches. They were both loud and terribly vulgar. Every other word was an expletive. The journey was punctuated with swearing, spitting on the floor of the van and loud farting. There was no response from the officers. They were used to it. Peter was not.

The handcuffs were beginning to bite into his skin. He had unwittingly tightened them by twisting his hands and trying to get some tissue paper out of his breast pocket. He begged the officers in whispers to loosen them. They pointedly ignored him, pretending not to hear. Such cruelty! Such…such unbelievable hypocrisy! Innocent until proven guilty. What a joke! Here was the law, his protection, ignoring the very rights it was supposed to protect. The cuffs…digging in…Even if he was guilty – which he was not – wasn't he a human being with human rights? Were human rights not due to him simply by virtue of his humanity? And did not this shackling of his hands and feet, this refusal to ease his cutting discomfort just a little, this causing of unnecessary mental and physical anguish, constitute a violation of the 1984 Convention against torture and cruel, inhuman and degrading treatment?

That one's for the birds, motherfucker!

They stopped at a Hardees fast food place for their first meal, after about six hours on the road. Two plain hamburgers and a cup of water! The cuffs remained, so eating was painful and humiliating. Peter had to manoeuvre the sandwich out of the bag and its wrappings into his mouth. His appetite failed him. He threw it back in the bag. The other inmates eyed his sandwich like hawks.

"Ain't you gonna eat that?" one of them asked.

Peter ignored him. He had said very little so far. He was terrified they would pick on him once they recognised him as being a foreigner.

Peter could scarcely believe he was chained to a murderer and sitting across from a homicidal armed robber. He felt cornered, as if he was struggling for his life in the grip of desparadoes. Deeply fearful, he backed away as far as the window, trying to put as much distance between himself, the killer and the highwayman, who sat there casually discussing their violent criminal lives, including acts they intended to commit when and if they got out. It was as if Peter was not there.

"Man I chased that motherfucker all the way to his front door and I shot him 6 times. I sprayed that mo'fuckers brains all over the wall".

Peter closed his eyes and began to pray. "Hail Mary, mother most chaste, mystical rose, full of grace, the Lord is with thee…"

The discordant harrowing tales continued. No remorse, no shock, no, how could you? Instead the audience was curious to know what kind of gun it was. .25 calibre handgun! Or was

it a 38 special? And with that, the discussion drifted off psy-
chotically into an analysis of various types of handguns and their
effectiveness.

Along the way, they picked up more inmates. Small - time
punks, one - dimensional hustlers, country bumpkins, hog stomp-
ing hillbillies. The bus was nearly full and the detainees were all
talking loudly.

A hippie with shoulder length hair, tufts of mutton-chop whis-
kers and greasy shirt covered with food stains, was sitting across
from Peter. Compared to the rest, he was surprisingly well spoken. Peter responded positively to his attempts at conversation.

"So you're going to the dark heart of Ham County, eh?"

Peter nodded.

"You know what they say about Ham County?"

Peter whispered that he didn't know but was always interested
in hearing something new.

"Come on vacation, leave on probation".

The hippie grinned, showing dirty brown coffee stained teeth
inside a wide mouth. He reminded Peter of a frog puffing up for
an enormous croak.

Peter smiled back tightly, bracing himself. He didn't know
what the hippie was talking about and that made him even more
nervous. But at least he seemed polite.

"Tell me more", Peter said, his voice betraying a slight tremor
of alarm. Mentally he began to prepare himself for the worst.

The hippie nodded.

"It's the lock up county of America. Every evening, new arrivals
troop in. Law enforcement in Ham County is a business. The
government pays lots of dollars for each person sent up state. So
they encourage recidivism because there's money to be made and
investors have to get returns because they are shareholders in a
listed company. Ham County's prison industry has become one of
the darlings of Wall Street. And it ain't just Ham. Across America,
there's been a huge boom in private penitentiaries. With an an-

nual growth rate of 45%, the market share has tripled in a decade. Crime does pay".

He reached under his shirt with one cuffed hand and scratched his belly.

"Didja hear about the old woman and the parking meters?"

Lock up County of America! Peter was thinking fearfully of what the hippie had been telling him earlier and wasn't sure he particularly wanted to hear about some old lady.

The hippie frowned. He wanted to create drama and he wasn't getting the right reaction from Peter.

"I wasn't either until I heard the story. She was over 70 years old but they sent her to jail for a simple act of charity -- putting money into exhausted meters outside the courthouse so the cars wouldn't get ticketed or towed away. They charged her with obstruction of justice. That's Ham County for you".

The hippie scratched the end of his prominent nose and regarded Peter's startled expression with large probing eyes swivelling around in sockets that seemed to small to support them.

"Ham County is the most conservative area of the mid-west. Ironically, Ted Turner, founder of CNN, was born in Ham. It's also where Charles Manson, the mass murderer was born. Ham County regularly records some of the highest conviction rates among major urban counties across America. People are routinely brought in, given impossible bail conditions and locked away for anything and everything. Lives and families are regularly destroyed. It's s system that's run amok and the people are largely unprotected".

There was a pause while Peter digested everything he had just been told. A monstrous image conjured itself up in his mind's eye. The hippie smirked, satisfied he was making an impression.

"To keep their judicial system working, they need criminals. If you ain't one they'll make you one. That's why we say 'come on vacation, leave on probation'. It's a German town and they use German nazi concentration camp surrender tactics. When they arrest you for example, your charge is trumped up. Instead of one count, you suddenly find you have two or three. This puts fear in you. They strip you and then they freeze you. Then they starve you and by the time you go in front of the judge, they say I have a deal for you. Because you are afraid, cold and hungry, before you even know what the deal is you take it, just to get out of it. That's what I call old fashioned surrender tactics".

Peter said he had never heard such stories before.

"We're talking cop out county here", the hippie continued. "It's the county with one of the highest conviction rates in America. And both the state and federal governments pay them for it. It's a business and to keep it going they have to feed more and more people into the system. That's why all they want is to convict you. They don't care how they get it. If people were charged properly and treated fairly they'd never have such a high conviction rate. But because they treat you so unfairly, you'll sign anything to cop out -- to get out. They say '"We've got a deal for you. In exchange for pleading guilty we'll credit you with time served. All you have to say is 'I'm guilty'". You don't want to spend another 90 days locked up so you agree whether you did it or not".

"Did you know you have to pay thirty dollars for your own arrest? Did you also know that you are not allowed to pay child support directly to your child or her mother? It's a legal scam. You have to pay it to the court, which keeps part of it in an interest bearing account and additionally charges you more dollars for processing before they then pass the balance on to the mother or guardian. If you paid directly to your child's mother, they wouldn't allow it. You'd have to pay it all over again. What you already paid would be considered a gift, not child support. Did you know all this about Ham County, man?"

Peter said he didn't but that from what he said, it seemed to him that child support laws had nothing to do with helping the child or preserving families, but everything to do with dollars.

"That's right. Now you're getting the picture. America is a money bags democracy". More like *dem all crazy*, Peter said, recounting the famous quip from the Nigerian Afro beat star, Fela Kuti.

Peter thanked the hippie for sharing his stories.

"You're welcome, England. At least now you've got all the dope", he added reassuringly. He yawned and closed his eyes. Peter took that as a signal the chat was over.

Alone again, thoughts of the things he'd just heard filled Peter with dread and deepened his depression. *They strip you and then they freeze you and starve you!* Breakout ideas and decampment schemes and escape plans competed with each other, fighting to colonise his head, each trying to provide a solution, each examined and discarded. *A German town using German nazi concentration camp surrender tactics!* Peter sat there on that iron rack, listening to the dull ache of despair inside him, feeling it grow like a balloon, suffocating him, forcing him to abandon all hope. No question about it, he was really in a pickle.

Four more gruelling hours to Tennessee! The chains prevented much movement. The smell of unwashed bodies was overpowering, the sight of puddles of spit around his manacled feet sickening. Nausea! Claustrophobia! Fear! Paranoia! Peter closed his eyes. He was so frightened and alone he could hardly breathe. He felt a rush of tears. He fought them. He could not be seen to be crying. Later when blessed darkness enveloped everything, he would set them free. But for the moment, he tried to visualise a better, happier world. Juliet's face drifted into view. *Oh my heart, my soul, my love!*

The mobile jail picked up another inmate, a 60 year old Italian American and big time Mafia drug dealer, jailed for 20 years. Meanwhile the killer Peter was chained to had fallen asleep, snoring loudly, smelly mouth agape, dribbling. He had squashed Peter into a compact area. Peter was trapped on the left by the killer's heaving, foul body and on the right by metal bars. He wiggled around, shifting to try to get more comfortable. The hand and leg cuffs tightened their cruel grip.

Peter suddenly developed a persistent itch in a place he could not reach and would much rather not mention aloud. He was driven insane by a desire to scratch. He had no choice but to remain where he was. He felt helpless. His wrists were raw and swollen. The handcuffs were fighting his every move. The leg shackles angrily restrained him. The major problem was that bloody leash with which they bound him to the killer. Peter could not move around without jerking him about too. At one stage, the killer cursed loudly and growled at Peter.

"Sit still motherfucker. I'm trying to get me some sleep in this mo'fucker".

Peter silently obeyed. Ten minutes later, pins and needles. Further *cautious* twisting and turning. To no avail!

Suddenly, the bus exited the motorway and pulled into a tiny county jail in Wartburg, Tennessee. It was a small hick town in the middle of nowhere. Population 900! The doors of the bus swung open.

"Alright, come on out for a piss and a stretch", said the male officer. Relief, but not for long.

The killer wanted to do a number two. The umbilical chain linking him to Peter would not be removed. Peter stood with his face and body half-turned away, less than two feet from him as he sat and defecated loudly. The stench was incredibly strong. Peter could feel vomit rising from his belly. He forced himself to swallow it down. His fear of the killer and what he might do were much greater than his sickness.

A flush! It was over. And now it was Peter's turn to urinate. With his hands cuffed, he tried to unzip his trousers to pass water. Pain shot through his wrists as he struggled to reach his underwear. His penis was half in and half out, bent into an impossible angle. He could no longer hold back. Piss -- forked -- shot out. One stream ran all over the rim of the toilet. The other trickled down his trousers. He no longer cared. Blessed relief washed over him. He had held back for several hours. He cared only to relieve his tortured bladder.

He managed to get his dick back into his underwear. It was

not possible to fully zip up. So he left it half-open. Getting half out of his trousers had been difficult. Getting back into it was almost impossible. The killer and Peter shuffled out.

Soon they were on the move again. Another inmate had come on board. The bus was tightly packed. Peter was in an even more compressed spot. Discomfort overwhelmed his body. Agony wracked his wrists and ankles. Mucus oozed despairingly from his nose, a cold or allergies or both, no tissues or handkerchief. Peter feared the consequences of one of his titanic sneezing fits. *If they can do this to you when you are innocent until proven guilty, what happens if you are found guilty? In any case, why should people who are innocent until proven guilty be locked away, shackled and humiliated while their accusers, who have to establish burden of proof, walk free?*

"God", Peter whispered, "if this doesn't end soon I'll die".

Juliet's face drifted into view. Peter clung to it for a hot second. Then he faded into merciful sleep.

They had been travelling for 16 hours. Peter no longer had any idea what day or time it was. It didn't matter anyway. He felt something rumbling from the depths of his stomach. It thrashed about then rose like a hideous worm, racing up, up, up till it reached his throat and lodged itself there. Nausea! Wild mood swings! His temperament became changeable, altering from minute to minute, in a state of perpetual flux, forming and re-forming perceptions and feelings with alarming rapidity: positive and negative, faithless and faithful, irritation and calm, laughter and sadness, despair and delirium. A tessellated succession of emotions at once connected to one another and yet detached from each other -- memories, thoughts, feelings, moods, actions, decaying in bitter, angry dissonance, fuelled by paroxysms of uncertainty.

The ultimate prize – a permanent anchor on CNN -- had been so close, virtually within his grasp. Then suddenly it had eluded him, as though he had been dreaming all along and just as he was about to grasp his winnings, he woke up to his fall from grace. *His* fall from grace!   It sounded so scary, so calamitous, so absolute and monstrous.   *The horned beast falling at the speed of light from the heavens.   Despatched, banished from the light into the darkness, into the pit of the dragon, the belly of hell.*

Peter tried to visualise the face of the prosecutor who had killed his dream and to stick voodoo pins into him.   *Calling all Orishas and Babalawos and Santeros!* He began with a needle to sow up the man's trap, ending with his eyes which he particularly enjoyed putting out.   He fantasised about crushing him like an insect.

The bus pulled into a local jail in Kentucky for a rest and some food.   Four hours of attempted kip in a crowded cage occupied by vagrants and malcontents.   The thought of sleeping in there with *them* was too horrible to contemplate.   So Peter sat in a far corner and catnapped.

A quick shower and some stale bread and porridge for breakfast.   Then, manacled and chained, with his spirit bowed, they began the last leg of the journey to Ham County.   As they gobbled up the miles, Peter wondered apprehensively what darker calamity he was about to encounter.   He felt like he was making the final descent into the lower world of Tartarus, the sunless abyss of torment and misery, where a more callous infliction upon his soul awaited.

THE JUSTICE CENTRE

Just before 5.00pm, the mobile cage crossed a bridge on the Ohio River into Cincinnati, entering the city at the Serpentine Wall – a border marking the divide between the rolling, endlessly wooded hills of Kentucky in the southern United States and the flattened farmlands of Ohio in the mid-west. Peter had learned in geography class at that boarding school "crammer" founded by the very austere Englishman, the Reverend Robert Fisher, that during the Ice Age, valley and continental glaciers flowing from the north carved out massive lake basins in areas around northern Ohio, Michigan, Lake Erie and the tip of northern Pennsylvania. These rather large masses of ice eventually melted away, leaving behind a great number of lakes and pools and vast expanses of fertile topsoil. But not before they had flattened most of the northern half of the Ohio Basin. The southern bit, part of an area known as the Bluegrass Region that extends from Cincinnati into central Kentucky, missed being glaciated and instead of being flat is rolling with hills and bluffs.

Cincinnati is the southernmost of the Ohio cities. It was founded in 1788 by soldiers who fought in the American War of Independence from Britain and originally named it "Losantiville". Two years later, in honour of General George Washington, a hero of the Revolutionary War, the name was changed to Cincinnati, after *Cincinnatus,* a famous Roman general who saved his realm then retired.

Peter had last been in Cinti as it was affectionately called (although Peter at that moment felt nothing but a violently negative disaffection for the city) fifteen years ago as a student at Xavier University, the so-called "Harvard of the Midwest", part of a clutch of first rate, liberal arts, private Jesuit universities that include Georgetown University in Washington DC, and subsequently as a news presenter on Xavier's campus radio and later still, as the news director of a commercial radio station.

As they drove in, he could see the hilltop communities of

Mount Adams and next to it, Clifton, the most liberal part of the city, where Peter often danced to live reggae music at *Bogarts* from the likes of Peter Tosh, Toots and the Maytals and Steel Pulse, the air thick with the smell and intoxication of dozens of marijuana joints. The University of Cincinnati spread out from Clifton into the downtown business district, which was built like a grid around Fountain Square at 5th and Vine streets.

Peter recognised the names of some of the other streets -- Race, Reading, Victory Parkway, Columbia Parkway, 6th, 8th. Cross streets numbered and designated east or west by their relation to Vine street. Wide streets, broad enough to take those yachts and submarines the Americans liked to call cars. Not like the narrow straitjacket streets back in England -- roads built for horses and carriages.

A German town using German nazi concentration camp surrender tactics!

They turned down one of the numbered roads and then up Sycamore street. There before them stood the Justice Centre, awesome, frightening and imposing, a structure designed to intimidate and subdue. Where *they strip you and freeze you and starve you! And where I'm gon' keep you!*

They were driven down a ramp to the Justice Centre's basement. Peter was jump hustled into the building, still manacled hand and foot. He found himself in a series of rooms separated by a long corridor on one side and glass doors and cubicles on the other. Corrections officers, regular police and plain-clothes detectives, their belted waists swelling outwardly and irregularly with all kinds of equipment designed to keep those arrested in check and those who do the arresting protected, moved between the hallway and the cubicles. Through an adjoining corridor, Peter made out a number of cells filled with mostly young black men and the occasional white face.

A fetid odour like rotting flesh hung in the air as Peter joined several other inmates who were lining up against a wall, waiting to be processed. All were handcuffed and those like himself who had been extradited from other cities or considered to be particularly dangerous also had leg chains. Most were black and young, in their late teens and early to mid twenties. A couple of them were middle-aged whites. They looked filthy and Peter guessed they were drunks or drug addicts.

By the time his turn came for processing ninety minutes later, Peter felt utterly exhausted. He suddenly realised that the foul stench was coming from him. His mouth had not been cleaned for nearly two days and it stank like a sewer.

Peter went through the motions: *name, address and age. Empty your pockets. Take off your shoes. Open your mouth lets see if anything's crawled up there. Spread your legs lets look up the crack of your arse. And while you're at it, cough lets see if anything pops out.*

A Corrections officer grabbed Peter's arm and marched him through the corridor to a brightly lit room. Big machines whirring away. A camera on one side, blinking. On the other, a monstrosity Peter later discovered to be a finger - printing machine. He was taken to the camera side first and positioned on a raised platform. Mug shots! Front and side! Then over to the monstrosity! Handcuffs removed! Fingers on the counter. Each one pressed into an inkpad then onto a computer pad. Finally, leg chains removed. It was finished. He had a new identity. He was inmate number 921870.

Down the corridor to cell no 8. Open cell bars! Peter went in and they shut behind him with a resounding crash.

"Welcome to America, England", the Corrections Officer said with a grin.

This was it. Trapped in the Justice Centre. Arrested, fingerprinted, photographed like a common criminal, a vagabond, then locked up without the possibility of escape. Peter counted about twenty doors that would have to be unlocked before he could get outside. Breaking out was out of the question. It would be like trying to break out of San Quentin or "the Rock". This was double *super* maximum security and he was stuck. They had control of him. Nothing he could do to change that. They were plugged into his system and had taken charge of his life -- a life he had not freely given up.

He had shifted from journalist to jailbird. *Six degrees of separation!* His life had been dominated by one great passion: to be one of the world's leading broadcast journalists. And he had all but achieved it. Then suddenly just when it was in his grasp, it was gone. His dreams, ambitions and development arrested by *them* because of a story told by her *of the Venus lips* turned *Venus flytrap.*

So, what had gone wrong? Why had the gods routed him, when it was clear he had been fated for great things? He felt a deep sorrow and bitterness that weighed him down and refused to allow him to be comforted.

I once existed, long long ago. I once lived and breathed and walked and talked just like everyone else. Just like every child I know, I once played in a school and in a garden and in a playroom and the vast outdoors, chased butterflies, caught insects, dissected lizards, planted seeds and watched fascinated as they began germinating the next day, played cowboys and Indians, went to amusement parks. And yes, loved ice – cream. My favourite always and for all time was vanilla. Plain and simple, with no mixes or extras, save occasionally for a burst of whipped cream or a chocolate stick. I sit here now, my face and voice cracked with grief, looking out with weak eyes, holding onto the memory of a boyish imagination I once had, remembering the moonlight games in the village, when we did not fear the night, before they came and took my soul away, before they murdered my life…

Peter looked around the cell and his heart almost died. It was packed. He was dangerously utterly alone, in the midst of a mob of strangers, an outsider sharing a banquet with the condemned. Guest of *dis*honour, invited to dine with the devil, an invitation he was not given the opportunity to refuse.

All eyes were on him, except the old white man in the corner who was snoring. Bored eyes. Staring at him. Rooting him to the spot. Hard mean faces. Recidivists without souls, who could hurt you because they were bored and had nothing else to do.

Peter shuddered. Him, *alone!* In the midst of a seething underworld, inhabited by the most unsavoury characters imaginable -- killers, rapists, armed robbers, petty thieves, drug dealers, drug addicts, child molesters, con artists, pimps. Him, *alone!*

They seemed to lose interest quickly except for one in particular whose complexion was dusky, obsidian black - *as night absent from light!* Beneath the protruding forehead, glittering heavily overcast eyes darted about, sinister and nervous. Predator sizing up his prey! Peter was a piece of meat -- wildebeest to a hungry lion in the Serengeti -- and *Koko* the brute was a predaceous animal without compassion.

Peter rested his eyes on *Koko* the brute. He looked like a cross between heavyweight boxers Joe Frasier and Mike Tyson, only meaner – looking. Powerfully built stunted arms, short legged, long bodied, like a dachshund.

Peter felt deepening apprehension as his eyes moved over that body. What a build! Tightly packed muscles rippling as he moved.

Koko the brute opened his mouth. Gold teeth flashed. He spat loudly in Peter's direction. Peter could hear the splat inches from his feet. The brute was grinning but it looked like a badger dog snarling.

"Punk ass English pussy," he said contemptuously, malevolently.

A thought crossed Peter's mind and before he could stop himself frustrated rage swamped caution and he said with unbelievable viciousness:

"I'm not English, I'm a British Nigerian, you idiot!"

Shock horror! What had he just said to *him* to whom the mighty steel-like arms belonged? The words seemed to have emerged from Peter's lips of their own accord. Unbidden! Somewhere in the part of his head where the limbic system joins the temporal lobe, a warning sign told him it was an unimaginably stupid thing to have said. But he'd gone right ahead and said it anyway and there was no going back now. His heart palpitated madly. His mouth felt parched.

Startled the brute stopped dead in his tracks. A look of utter astonishment appeared on his face. He seemed to be grappling with the fact that he had just been challenged but wasn't quite sure what to do. The realisation came as a shock to him.

He looked around but no one else appeared to have noticed. They were listening with interest to an inmate who was feeding them some sensational news about a recent killing. Holding court and loving the attention. *"I seen that motherfucker whack that bitch with a 38. Pow! And after that he just went back to watching fucking TV like nothing happened. Damn!"*

Peter took advantage of the pause and acted quickly -- a move that probably saved his life with seconds to spare. While the brute was standing there looking stunned, Peter hurried over to the steel doors and banged as loudly as he could. With a bellow of rage the brute lowered his head, *El Toro* preparing for the death charge. Peter looked into those glittering black eyes and was convinced his life was about to be wiped out. *If I were to have an epitaph, what would it be?*

Peter weaved aside just in time as the brute blundered past him into the wall. As he made to come back and finish the job, by a freak of astonishing coincidence that some would describe as a miracle, the cell door clanged open and caught him in the face, bringing him down with a mighty thud.

The Officer who responded to Peter's frantic banging on the door had no idea what had happened. Seeing the weakness and panic in Peter's eyes, he grinned sympathetically.

"You're lucky", he said. "We're just about ready to move you out to the pods. Or else they'da had your English ass for dinner. Come with me".

Out on the corridor, Peter gasped with relief, safe for the moment.

"Back against the wall", ordered the officer.

Peter sheepishly obeyed. Fear of what might have happened to him in *there* had turned him cold.

"They're placing you on suicide watch cos you ain't from here and they ain't sure what to expect. That means I'm placing you in solitary for twenty-four hours without no blankets or sheets. We got cameras watching you and shit so don't try nuthin' silly".

The pod was divided into single occupant cells. Inside each one there was a locker, a sink, a toilet, a mattress on a metal rack and nothing else. The one Peter was forced to occupy smelt of urine and foot rot, the kind of odour that comes out of soft soled, sweaty, pissed on canvas shoes worn without socks on a hot and humid day -- a damp, pissy, sweaty rotten smell.

It had been a long day and Peter was desperate for some sleep. But it was dreadfully cold in that pod and his head felt like it was being cryogenically frozen. The arctic air-conditioning blasted a frost that was a blessing for his allergies but a merciless punishment for his sinuses.

They'll freeze and starve you...Nazi concentration camp surrender tactics...

Peter developed a throbbing monster of a headache that gripped the inside of his ears. It felt like some very energetic African *Atilogwu* drummers had managed to convey themselves in a tiny vivarium into his brain and were now making an enormous insouciant racket, like the rush of a stampeding herd. He felt certain hidden remote cameras were observing all his actions. As if he was living his life inside a television set and the remote control was in the hands of ravening CO's who were now manipulating everything -- Big Brother, full of malevolence with a dark heart and a vile, evil disposition, marking Peter as an enemy of the state to be kept under close surveillance and on a given signal, be devoured voraciously by a plangent beast.

Peter sank deeper into piteous wretchedness. A small ductless gland at the base of his brain secreted a sudden powerful rush of phlegm, making him want to vomit. Fear, with a faltering sound, like quick light steps, whispered in his ears. What was happening to him? The realisation that he had no idea made him choke. Perhaps if he cried a little but he was too shocked to weep. He had always hated being manipulated by others, losing charge of his life. But that was precisely what had happened. They even had the asperity, the impudence to place him on suicide watch even though it was they who had created intolerable conditions that would make the intentional killing of one's self highly desirable to the weak minded. But they didn't want that mess on their hands so they froze and starved him and banged on his cell door every hour through the night, like wicked spirits who could not rest in peace but prowled the face of the earth causing mischief.

Who was he? What was he doing here in this unnatural place of forced exile and insecurity? The life outside had been capriciously severed. He could only live an inner life. The things he could no longer see he found within, heard in his heart.

Peter closed his eyes. Time stood still. *He waited, naked and alone. He heard a faint rustle. He sensed a presence. Juliet! Don't leave! Tarry awhile! Hold onto my name. Keep me sacred. Guard me, lest I lose myself in this room full of snakes. Sit down with me on this rack. Would you like to hold my hand? A delicate smile! You were here! Something wonderful happened. He didn't dare move.*

Peter opened his eyes and a living, benumbing death came to him. Dark hearted, red-clawed. It trapped him, chained him, muffled him, weighed him down and forced him to lose sensation, to become dull and lustreless. How long was he to be locked down like this?

Time stretched! Merciless time! Oh to see beyond the here and now. How to escape from this cage of horrors?

He prayed for deliverance away from the rats and snakes and danger and dark hearts and red claws and malevolence and chains and traps and living death.

Deliverance did not come. *My father won't come and get me*

-- his little girl's voice, speaking to him -- *Now you know what it feels like to be abandoned, you naughty, naughty, Daddy!* The morning was bad. Peter was back in his unfamiliar world, assaulted by a range of emotions and feelings he didn't know existed in him. A never-ending carousel ride, where the operator had started the ride and left his post and Peter had no way of getting off. It was amazing that he could have such a wide range of emotions and still keep his sanity. But for how long?

Peter woke up full of remorse, a gurgling sound like a death rattle in his ears, afraid to move, worried that any movement would further confirm what he already knew to be true -- that he was trapped in a strange city, caged amongst a strange tribe of people, in a strange country. He felt nothing but the cold, suffocating hands of despair and disheartenment crawling up his body, consuming him totally, submerging him in a lake of hopeless gloom.

The voice of the guard cracked like a whip, forcing him to get up or face the wrathful consequences, exploding in his head at 5am, the day stretching ahead, another day in captivity, absolute hopelessness in Yank country, a British Nigerian "deadbeat" in Cincinnati, trapped in an unimaginably gross, inexpressibly sad environment.

Breakfast! Little pink yellow and green things floated up to the surface after Peter stirred the porridge. Oats mixed with...coleslaw? He tasted it. *Doorsteps* and *dishwater!* Disgust welled up inside him but he forced it down hungrily. Afterwards, he felt sick from the slop. His stomach heaved with bilious ejection. He barely made it to the sink before a stream of vomit belched forth from inside him.

Throwing up didn't make Peter feel any better. He couldn't get his mind off that horrible meal. He felt worse but there was nothing left to bring up and discharge in him. His stomach rolled and rumbled as he staggered to his bed. *Oh God! If you are going to do it, let it be now. This is the best time to die.*

But he survived and by mid-morning, the ejection was pushing south and Peter felt a great need to visit the lavatory. His stomach heaved and groaned. He had already lost his breakfast. Now he felt in danger of losing his guts. He felt sick as a poisoned dog. But he was also savagely hungry and the need for food exhausted him. He longed for some real British fare: baked beans on toast, marmalade, fried tomatoes, British bacon and sausage, fish and chips dripping with vinegar and chip shop curry, lamb chops with brown sauce and mushy peas. He even missed marmite, something he rarely ate. And real Nigerian grub: pepper soup with dried and stock fish, jollof rice with chicken and plantain, pounded yam with okra soup and beef, garri with egusi and fresh fish, ukazi with goat meat and ground rice.

By late morning, Peter thought he was going to pass out from hunger. He felt a malnourished discomfort, a punishing craving he didn't think possible. Fortunately, lunch came early. It was shockingly bad. It consisted of a few slices of bread and watery soup with bits of pasta and vegetables and other unidentified floating objects. The Sloppy Joe's looked like a mixture of coloured water, mucus and bits of mince- meat. The potatoes looked diseased and unnaturally bloated. Peter found the mere sight of the food, if he could call it that, repulsive. But he was hungry and forced himself to wolf it down.

Peter never got used to jailhouse fare. Detainees lived on pints of milk, and were fed "cat food" -- yucky slop that you sucked on rather than chewed and kept your energy level low and manageable for the guards. Being carnivorous to the core, Peter daily longed for a piece of real steak.

As they stood in a queue to return the plastic trays, a scruffy looking inmate with plaits who was standing behind Peter began to cough. A deep, rumbling, phlegm-filled cough! Cursing, the inmate spat against the wall. Unfortunately, Peter happened to look in that direction at the same time and saw the blob as it hit the wall. His stomach heaved. *Oh God, please don't let me throw up in here.* The fellow began to cough again. Peter turned and looked at him briefly, hoping his eyes would say it all, English like.

The bloke reacted angrily.

"What the fuck is you looking at bitch? I got manners. I covered my mouth. Damn! You don't got to look at me that way, motherfucker".

And he spat again against the wall.

Late afternoon. The loudspeaker inside Peter's pod crackled into life.

"England, pack your shit. You're going to Queensgate".

The cell door was opened automatically by remote. An inmate on outside detail wheeled a trolley full of blue uniforms down the hallway, stopping at every cell.

"What size?" he asked impatiently. Before Peter could reply he said "2X" and tossed a two-piece uniform at him.

Minutes later, dressed in detention blue, ten detainees including Peter were marched single file into a recreation room equipped with fixed round tables and stools and a television set. Twenty others were already in there, collecting their kit, which consisted of stone mattress, pillow, blanket, 2 sheets, toothbrush, toothpaste and a piece of soap -- standard issue.

Peter picked up his pile and headed for the corner. Several eyes were watching him. He noticed some of them were looking at him as if he was diseased -- something to avoid. Then he saw they were looking at his shoes without the laces. Everyone knew immediately that he was on suicide watch.

One of them was casting furtive, sideways glances at Peter. Then suddenly his eyes flashed with recognition.

"Hey brother, I seen you on Tee Vee men. You dat deadbeat motherfucker from England, ain't you?"

"They got your face on all them news programmes", another one said.

Yet another: "My sister seen you in the newspaper in Hollywood. You a star deadbeat dad".

"You on America's most wanted".

"They say you the worst deadbeat dad in America".

They all laughed and like little children, promptly turned their attention to something else. Their minds were once again empty blackboards. But not before they had scornfully, insolently, contemptuously fired an arrow through Peter's pride with this public abuse.

Peter sighed gloomily, but kept his shoulders squared, his head high. Outwardly defiant and in command of himself. But inside, shrivelled up, grief stricken.

Deadbeat dad! All his achievements, his hopes, his dreams reduced to such vulgarity by these hicks. *Deadbeat dad!* His personal life on parade, his dirty laundry hanging out for all to see! The threads of his life -- shredded. Everything, going, going, whirling, whirring fast! Real fast! Nothing left to do but mourn the death of his life, the Peter he once knew, filling him with a deep, dark, drear grief.

The uncomfortable lump in Peter's throat was so large it threatened to choke him. He realised he was no longer invisible. This herd of misfits, this great flowing tide of dissolute creatures forcibly bound together had recognised and set him apart. Something huge had suddenly entered their tiny, provincial lives -- like an *alien* invasion, the same term, it occurred to Peter, used by the American government to officially describe foreigners.

Peter lapsed into a troubled silence. He had the incredible sensation of being engulfed by a thick shadow of apprehension. Thought after thought after thought raced through him, crowding his mind, quickening his pulse, causing blood to pound his temples. *Will I ever get out of here? Will I make it through the next hour, never mind the day?*

Peter felt like he was dreaming. It was as if time stood still. But it was actually the clock that appeared to stand still. It was ticking all right, but slowly. He was sure that outside, beyond the thick walls – the windowless walls of this cage in the Justice Centre -- he was sure that the day was progressing inexorably, morning advancing into afternoon, evening gradually being stained by darkness, becoming night. But inside, in the lost world of this American nick, under this crepuscular light, the only indication of change and of a new day was the ticking of the clock and he could hear it was not beating as it should.

Endless minutes crept by deceptively, pretending to be seconds but lasting for hours. One minute became an hour. One hour lasted six hours. Six hours became his long night. His long night became an endless night. The endless night turned into a dark interminable age. The dark age immersed his being in the dumps. The dumps forced his whole person to crumble, decline and become a mere fraction of what he had been.

The face of the *woman* faded into view.

Who are you? Why have you turned my world upside down?

Presently, the tannoy crackled into life.

"Okay, genlmen, pick up your shit, the bus is here and you're off to Queensgate".

They trooped in single file into the bus, clutching their sparse belongings. Peter felt odd in the two piece blue uniform, his blanket, pillow and mattress sticking out awkwardly in front of him and from under his arms. No one, least of all himself, could have believed that just a few weeks ago, he had the entire world watching him on CNN, listening to his every word. Today he was just like any other inmate, stripped of his dignity, strip-searched, the world locked away behind him, *a world of carnal desires and lustful transgressions* that had brought him to this queens hole with a secure gate.

QUEENSGATE

A ten-minute bus ride later, the detainees were marched into Queensgate Correctional Facility, a dismal eight story building that was originally built as a warehouse. It was now a human factory, a lock up facility where inmates ate, slept and vegetated in states of stultifying boredom and near insanity. Inside, it felt to Peter like a loony bin with its off-white, windowless walls and confusing network of disinfected corridors.

The passageways were all inter-linked. Peter and the rest of the new arrivals marched past a stairwell and down long, white-washed corridors that narrowed into a corner antechamber, then widened into the dining hall also known as the "chow" hall, before skirting around the commissary and medical centres and giving onto the admissions vestibule. Everywhere, phosphor lamps, radiating ultra violet light and mercury vapour, left a stark, dreadful brightness.

At admissions, the detainees listened to a stern speech from a tall Corrections Officer. *You are all cheques. We lock your ass up and then we make you pay for it. Your arrest is going to cost you thirty dollars. When I call your name, git down here and sign over your thirty bucks...*

His words reminded Peter of the Chinese who executed condemned prisoners with a single bullet and then made their families pay for it.

The CO separated the detainees into groups of ten. Peter and his detachment were marched down the hallway into a lift, watched by dozens of security cameras. They ascended to the 7th floor.

There were about 120 detainees on the 7th level, split into two wings that were separated by a common room, like Peter's old boarding school dormitory in eastern Nigeria. The sleeping cage, for that was what it was, had screened windows, just like those box windows of the Remove dormitories at Government College,

Umuahia and – his brain went into action suddenly in a moment of escapist fancy from his tortured present – the dormitories looked like frat houses and were called Fisher, Kent, Cozens, Wareham, Simpson, New, School, Niger, Nile and of course Extension House where Bob "the Antelope" used to live. And Extension House was situated across from the quadrangle and Bob who happened to be a bit of a bounder was always having narrow escapes with the House Master whose office sat directly opposite the House entrance and who could scent you even before he saw you through that Remove box window. And now Peter could see in his mind's eye that promiscuous village tart from the eatery across the road known as Madam Shack, the area local slut with the heavy lisp and thick posterior who smelled of insects and who eventually screwed half the third form at tuppence each. But Bob the stud had been the first to get in there. True to type he had fearlessly brought her into the dormitory late one night after lights out and Peter recalled the terrific wanking gratification from observing their writhing naked bodies through the secret vantage point of those Remove box windows. But he also remembered with a shudder the experience of damn near splitting a gut when the lookout, that affable chap, nicknamed "Navajo Joe" from Fisher House, came rushing past the windows yelling "housemaster alert" at the same time as the door of the dorm swung open and the housemaster stood there, but failed to notice anything unusual in that darkened dormitory.

Except those boarding school screened windows were designed to protect while these ones he was now observing, as his mind came juddering back to the present, had been made to keep him in lock down, to throw him into a state of purgatory. These ones he now slowly dizzily discerned and that had him reeling from shock and set his heart beating unpleasantly. These ones had *bars*, huge teeth clamed together with lips permanently drawn off in what seemed to Peter to resemble a sick grin.

The path they were treading ran them through a hostile gauntlet of reprobates -- crack users and dealers, petty thieves, street smart con men, pimps, robbers, probation violaters, sex fiends, fraudsters -- all sorts. Jaded, malevolent eyes, following them as they fell in behind the guard taking them to assigned corners.

Most of the inmates -- about 80 percent -- were young and black, with an incredible variety of hairstyles. Watching the coiffure in motion was a strange sight. They were quiffed and combed into the most bizarre shapes and sometimes swayed as their owners walked. As people moved, huge hedges of hair followed them. Some were piled high like hillocks. Others were platted mohawks. Some cascaded down in huge bleached dreadlocked knots, like long golden icicles and stalagmites in motion. Some looked like matted 60's wigs. Others were in ponytails or Afros. Some heads were as clean-shaven as polished glass, reflecting gleams of fluorescent light. Others tresses were cut short in the front and left long in the back, like mullets. Some of them looked as if they were about to take off.

The inmates almost always had their hands down the front of their trousers, engines rumbling on horse power, stroking or thigh slapping or just holding onto their *schlorts*. It was as if some unseen force, which for some bizarre reason was speaking with a Teutonic Scottish accent in Peter's thoughts, was urging them to *whip out yer wangs and go ter town...*

Armed with their *schlediums*, they walked or rather rolled with a much affected strut -- the pimp roll -- some more affected than others, making them appear to hop, skip and jump, rather than walk. It was funny to see even older men, some of them in their sixties, doing the pimp roll. One such with a malefic grin and no teeth walked with a limp. He would mumble greetings to Peter, *"Hey, whatcha' know good England"*, as he dragged his bad leg, rolled his shoulders and affected a sideways scuttle like a giant break-dancing crab.

Peter noticed that most wore their trousers not around their waists but at the base of their bottoms. He felt sure that if they could, some of them would have worn them around their ankles. He later learned that like the hands in their pants situation, it was a street macho affectation which was started by gang members. "Don't mess with me" sort of thing. They wore their trousers "half staff" for the same reason they had gold fixings in their teeth -- to show they were drug dealers, which on the streets is seen as a terrifically hip thing to be. You showed you were making money by filling your teeth with gold.

3

_____

PETER FOUND HIS RACK -- bed 88 -- made up the bed and collapsed onto his back. He stared up at the ceiling. It had all kinds of pipes and lighting fixtures and what appeared to be a soft loose paper padding, some sort of toxic ash drizzling to earth in the form of dust particles, keeping everyone sneezing.

Hours passed. Outside, darkness approached. Inside, Peter was in gloom. He stared up at the pipes and vents running across the rough ceiling. He turned on his side. In front of him he could see through the barred windows, out beyond the courtyard, past the trees overhanging the main road, beyond the street lights and the houses dotting the elevated landscape and over the hills of Kentucky, gateway to the south.

His back was turned to the television viewing area. But he could hear and smell the corruption behind him. Rotting humanity, freaking out over a wrestling match on TV. Unlike Peter, they seemed relaxed and comfortable, locked away in this cage, cursed to return again and again. A lifetime of cages! Life in a hole!

11pm! Lights out! Peter was lying on his stomach, trying as best as he could to get comfortable. The mattress was as hard as stone. It felt as if he was lying on the concrete floor. He drifted in and out of sleep. Several times he woke up shivering. The cage was freezing and the blanket was exceedingly thin. If this was summer, how could one hope to survive winter in this place? Peter perished the thought. There was no way he would be here for that long.

Beyond his sleeping rack, nothing stirred the quiet apart from the hum of the air conditioner, a distant snore, a loud fart, the occasional crackle of the CO's walkie talkie.

Peter was lulled into dreaming. The voice of the stranger was powerful, drawing him irresistibly to it. Peter leaned forward, laid his face against the barred windows, felt nothing but the chill of the night air. The windows and bars were gone. The voice, deep and sonorous, beckoned. Peter removed his slippers and stepped into the night, dropping himself off the edge into the foggy night, into free fall. Down seven floors through the misty blackness. Peter could see nothing but the stranger's hands far below, glowing eerily. He fell slowly like a parachute, the glowing hands directing him, urging him away from the cage of steel.

A flash! Peter awoke not into the warm luminosity of the strangers' arms, but into the cold embrace of lost, esurient souls. Every bone felt broken. The air was stiff. The light was harsh. The fairy tale was over. The dream locked away.

Snap! Snap! Snap! Startled, Peter caught his breath. His brow knitted tightly. It was the sound of those horrible, hateful lights coming on, signalling the end of quiet time. Time to rejoin the raging throng. A feeling of sad dismay washed all over him.

Peter woke into his first morning at Queensgate and wondered to himself what would happen when he stepped into the morning of the outside world to begin his life once more. Would it still be familiar or would it have been so altered as to be invisible to him, like a sojourner returned after a long period away? Would she, the one that had possession of his heart, still remember him after this absent courtship? Peter forced himself to blunt out the thoughts.

Bray! Bray! Bray! The CO's voice on the speakers sounded like a donkey braying. "Genlmen, we are second for chow. Giddup, make your beds, brush your teeth, wash your faces. And when you git down there, keep your hands atta your pants, no talking in the chow hall…"

Bark! Bark! Bark! Now his colleague was a raging mastiff, warning of dire consequences if anyone failed to obey orders. Peter was never quite sure whether he was saying "chow time" or "count time". His face – monolith, mirthless -- could have been carved out of stone.

It was just 5am but already the din had begun. The voices of resentful men -- swearing, cursing, praying, singing -- could be heard rising cacophonously above the sleeping racks and up to the ceiling, before descending ferociously on all those who were still trying to steal a few extra winks, forcing them to rouse from their sleepy-eyed reveries. The voices rose and rose and rose and then rolled down to earth in thick waves that consumed the sleepers, submerging them in dense noise until they were forced to rise or drown in the din.

To Peter's reckoning, the inmates did everything loudly: belched, farted, shat, snored, coughed, spat and cursed loudly. A loud people with clamorous habits! It had to be the result of an innate childishness that was in all of them, white or black. Why they couldn't at least try to do it quietly beat the pants off him. Peter would be in a lift filled with people and suddenly directly behind him, a conspicuously loud filthy belch would explode, from the very sewer of hell itself. Other times they would yawn and cough directly into his face. *What is the spread pattern of your cough? Couldn't you at least put your hand over your mouth?* One guy spat onto the railings right next to Peter as he went down for supper. *What rubbish heap did they dig you out from?* Ignorant, loud, uncouth, unpleasant, shocking louts, with their laughable hairdos and pimp rolls.

In spite of all the noise, most new arrivals including Peter were unprepared for the early morning wake up call to breakfast at 5.00am. Everyone without exception felt, looked and smelled horrible in that early hour. People sleepwalked, bumping into each other as the breakfast queue made its way towards the counter.

"Look where you're going in this bitch, bitch!"

"Sorry man! Damn! I'm still sleeping like a mo'fucker".

The breakfast queue snaked all the way down the length of the hall for about a hundred yards. Troops in blue! Legion of vice! It made Peter think of some affirmative action youth programme. A few whites, Asians and Hispanics were sprinkled liberally down the line, but to Peter's unaccustomed eye, it looked as if the entire young black male population in Cincinnati was banged up in there.

Peter soon discovered that food from the dining hall was strictly to be eaten in the hall and not taken to the sleeping cage, except for oranges and provisions purchased from the commissary. The porters were the only ones allowed to consume their extra ration of bologna sandwiches in their corners as payment for their work.   Black inmates often looked down on the porters whom they accused of working for the white jailers. They nicknamed them "house niggers" and even parodied a Donna Summer hit song after them:

"We work hard for bologna…so hard for bologna…"

Like most inmates, Peter hated the chow hall regime that allowed you only about five minutes to gulp down your meal. People often tried to smuggle bread and hot dogs, cold drinks and the like back to their floors.

"You see how those bill collectors try to get blood out of stone?" barked the fat, dog-faced officer, jowls shaking.   "Well I'm going to show you how to get a milk carton out of *Nike*".

Mirth exploded across the hall as he reached down and pulled out a small carton of milk from beneath the velcro strap of an inmates trainers. He raised his hand in triumph.

"It's a few days in the hole for you buddy and a warning to the rest of you. Keep the chow in the chow hall. Tuck your shirts in. Let your dicks go and keep your mouths shut".

One of the reasons officers demanded absolute silence in the dining hall was because they wanted to do away with or at least control distractions such as queue jumping. *Line jumpers* as they were popularly known were those who would go two or three times down the queue during meals and pick up several trays of food. Corrections staff argued they would not be able to feed all the inmates if this continued to happen, but in truth, they often threw extra food away. For their part, the inmates complained that the rations were too small.

One fellow jumped the line 110 times in a space of three weeks. When he was finally caught, everyone cheered him and he became a hero. As punishment, they woke him up every morning at 3.00 and made him wash all the pots and pans for a couple of weeks.

Something else that caught Peter's attention was the system of bartering inside the dining hall. As soon as the food trays were picked up the exchange in trade began -- one commodity for another -- reaching a heated pace very quickly.

"I've got eggs for cake", "milk for grits", "bread for potatoes", "sugar for salt", "oatmeal for pancakes".

Peter felt like he had strayed into a thriving *Suq* bazaar. It was a hustle and it got most of the inmates quite excited. The guards generally looked the other way.

Some of the inmates took it beyond the dining hall and into the sleeping cage where people would walk from rack to rack, trading pencils for pens, underwear for potato crisps, envelopes for coffee. It was like being in an age before money was invented.

4

THE MAIN DUTY OF the Corrections Officers or CO's was to take custody and control of the inmates. They had been trained not to trust the inmates and to second - guess everything. During their "rookie" phase, they were made to believe that everyone in jail was no good and Peter saw them looking around with hostility and suspicion. The attitude of the inmates didn't help much either. They demonised anyone in uniform, targeting them for abuse.

It was especially tough on the new recruits. Fresh faced, young, slightly apprehensive if not downright scared, the rookies were almost invariably white. And since the inmates were mostly blacks and in the majority, the rookies made easy targets for abuse. Their mere entry into a recreational area elicited the most vitriolic contempt. "Come and get it fool!" "Through your ass hole bitch!" "Fuck you hill billy", were some of the more respectable expletives the guards had to endure. As the new recruit attempted to assert his authority over a particularly unruly character, cat - calls and a torrent of racist taunts would explode from the far side. He would turn crimson, to the absolute delight of his tormentors.

The younger officers, aged below forty-five and making up more than half the total number of CO's, all wore their hair close-cropped and were packed with muscle, not to be trifled with. The rest – chubby cheeked, beer bellies hanging over their uniformed trousers – were overweight. With their droopy eyes, wobbly jowls and wattled throats, they reminded Peter of recovering drunks. When they spoke it always came across uncannily as if they were barking. It seemed they did this on purpose to scare the inmates, attempting to make up with their voices what the years had un-kindly taken from their bodies.

Peter found that a few of the more senior officers were quite approachable, often sympathising with the plight of the inmates. Most CO's however would go out of their way to make life un-comfortable, flaunting their authority, kicking you when you were down, violating you, hurling insults at you. Their barked commands and abuse of power filled Peter with unspeakable fear and resentment.

Take visiting for example, which happened three days a week at one visit per day lasting approximately 15 minutes. Inmates spent more time waiting to be taken up after each visit -- some-times up to one hour -- than they did with their visitors, simply because the guards couldn't be bothered.

Inmates were always waiting. To go to court for a ten-minute hearing, you spent an average of six hours waiting in the "bull pen". To go to commissary to pick up provisions you paid for, something that usually took less than five minutes, you spent on average 45 minutes to an hour waiting in a queue to be taken down and another 30 minutes waiting to come back up. This was not official policy of course, more the cruelty of the guards. You were essentially at their mercy. Often times you would be asked to queue up in front of the stairway and just wait, for no justifiable reason, while the CO's played cards or chatted with one another. If you complained, they would book you for unruly behaviour, which meant several days in the hole, the catacombs where they bury you alive. Or worse, they could take you into the lift, accuse you of attacking them and beat you to a pulp.

The 11pm to 7am "graveyard" shift was the most dangerous time -- the shift where "anything can happen" as Peter's new corner mate, Lovell, put it. He was a skinny 39-year old crack addict with vacant eyes who had violated his probation.

"Officers on the graveyard shift is easily the meanest motherfuckers, maybe cos they gat to sit through the night", Lovell told Peter. "They took this one guy downstairs during this shift. He had an argument with a guard. He refused to shuddup after several warnings. So a group of officers came and took his ass downstairs to the hole. He never came back up. The next morning they say he kill his self. But I believe that 'cos he had a lot of mouth, they probably beat him to death, know what I'm saying, killer?"

Peter's brain went cold. How could he possibly cope? He was a creature born of another world. *Dear God, thanks for all the hints. I think I've got the message and can infer the correct meaning of your inspired clues. Can we now suspend hostilities? Please?*

Not only did Peter have to worry about vicious inmates he also had to deal with sadistic officers. He witnessed brutality from the guards a number of times that was out of all proportion to the provocation.   He watched an officer dislocate an inmates arm simply because he barked an order and the detainee, who was at least twice his age, said very calmly:

"You don't gat to speak to me like that. All you gotta do is ask me to go to the elevator and I'll go. You ain't got to shout".

The officer freaked, grabbed him, flung him against the wall, cuffed him and twisted his arm viciously as he led him away. Peter cowered in fear.

The only way to escape the constant threat of violence was to get as far away from Queensgate as possible. But it wasn't like he could suddenly get up and just walk away. Why wasn't there a rulebook, a civil or human rights leaflet or something that spelled out what the guards could and could not do? After all, Peter reasoned, at least some of the detainees were innocent because their guilt was yet to be proven. They had already been cruelly humiliated and denied their freedom. Did they have to live under a violent dictatorship as well?

Lovell, Peter's corner mate looked around uneasily to make sure no CO was listening. "The reason we don't realise our rights are being violated", he whispered, "is 'cos they got our minds playing folly. They keep us playing cards and watching TV and shit and before we know it we go in front of the judge and we are sentenced and it's too late. All we know is what we've done. But ain't nobody telling us how to defend ourselves. All we've got are public defenders who hardly come to see us. They say we got to write to them, but how many black American men in here can write? Instead of having a hotline to reach the defenders, we have nuthin. They be using cruel punishment to break us. Court starts at 9am but we get woke up at 3am, taken to court and kept in cold, concrete chambers. All you can think about is what can I do to get out?"

"Why can't you lodge an official protest", Peter asks?

Lovell paused to collect his thoughts.

"You really are a foreigner ain't you?" he said, staring at Peter in disbelief. "Look at me men. I'm a crack addict. I ain't got a career or education. I ain't even got a home. All I got is a mouth full of gold and a butt full of dope. I advertise -- I'm the doughboy, catch me if you can. Ain't no question who is the gingerbread man. If you stay on that corner long enough, it'll catch up with you".

Peter wasn't sure he grasped everything he said, but he understood enough. They could not afford quality representation -- the type that would have made a fair trial possible. Nine times out of ten they were stuck with public defenders that operated like assistants to the prosecutors because they were state-appointed. They were not likely to go against the state because the state paid their salaries.

Statistically, the figures showed that if you were poor and black in America you were more likely to go to prison. 1 in 3 African American men between the ages of 14 and 25 are in US prisons and the largest number of people in those prisons -- up to 75 percent -- are black men.   In the year 2000, there were reportedly over a million black men in American prisons -- more than there were black people in American institutions of higher learning. As Peter found out, most inmates were poor, under-educated and black. This in a nutshell was why more blacks than whites ended up in the penitentiary.

Peter quickly discovered that there was no reference book for inmates' rights in jail or in court. What you had was the Revised Code, which was designed for two things: to tell you what you supposedly did and what you get for what you did.   It offered no suggestions on mitigation or litigation, nothing about how to defend yourself.

So the guards, who were mostly white, could literally get away with murder. It was rumoured by the black inmates that they were all members of the Ku Klux Klan. If this was true, it never manifested itself to Peter in any tangible way. With the exception of maybe one or two officers, they were either generally friendly or chose to ignore him completely.   Most felt he had no business being locked up with criminals and they faulted the system. A couple of them were fascinated with Peter, an African Brit with "that accent". For his part, Peter tried to be as affable with them as he could, knowing his safety depended on it. They never knew how scared and depressed he was. Sometimes it was so bad he felt dizzy.

5

AFTER BREAKFAST, PETER SAT staring through the barred windows. Puffy clouds drifting by. He felt a wave of resentful longing. To be a cloud, free to travel anywhere on earth. He focused on a particularly dark cloud.

There was so much free time. Time to do nothing. It deepened the pain of loneliness. Peter sat there on that misty morning, waiting for something -- anything -- to happen. Boredom crawled through him like worms. A train with a fitting name, *Con*rail, rolled past. Behind it an enormous junkyard of old broken down cars formed a bleak backdrop, like the scenery of a post nuclear war film set, completing the picture in Peter's mind of the Mad Max urban wilderness into which he had descended.

Across from Peter, a new arrival, a red neck with long, wild hair and ZZ Top beard, looked like all he needed was a staff and swaddling robes and you could rename him John the Baptist.

The sky suddenly turned grey and it started to drizzle. The low clouds depressed Peter and he cried hard into his pillow. He felt like a fish out of water. A man of his stamp, wretched and alone! Sod the Yanks and their sodding laws for screwing up his life. All sodding blighters! And right now their control over his destiny, their power over him or what was left of him. His life -- minute by minute, day by day -- had been colonised, taken over, struck down, rocked by a jittery, dreadful bilious fear that flowed through him with a splashy sound like the rain outside, drops of it hanging off the sides of his face and body like sweat, forcing his finger tips to quiver like autumn leaves in a breeze.

He had to keep his spirits up at all cost. Had to maintain indomitable fortitude in the face of this hideous nightmare, had to pull himself together. He was wired into one of the most re-spected families in Nigeria. Son of the good seed that germinates on good ground, the legal eagle himself. Born never to give in to pressure.

Peter wondered suddenly how his parents were taking it all. Much of his life he had spent in planning how he would make himself eminent in their eyes. And now this.

His mother would be worried sick. Peter had always been close to her. Often when he prayed and he thought of the Virgin Mary, it was his mother's face that floated up angelically before his eyes.

His father's disciplinarian face would be stern and grave, his mood quick-tempered in the manner of a high-achieving man who had little tolerance for human failings of any kind. *The shame of it! My son in an American nick! Never mind his innocence! Me, Justice of the Supreme Court, defender of the law, internation-ally recognised jurist, Knight of the Papal Realm, Commander of the Order of the Niger.* Peter could see the old man frowning in his study, his face filled with reproach, a pair of gimlet eyes bearing down sharply on Peter, drilling holes into him. The Pater, the Beak, brimming with disapproval, intoning wrathfully: *that which you are told to do, you will not do. It is that which you are told not to do -- cavorting with immoral, little women -- that is the one you will do. Filth! Dirt!*

And cavort Peter did. There had been all sorts over the years, to the old man's vexed disappointment -- tall, short, fat, thin, black, white, Asian, Latina and all shades in between. He'd met them in Europe, America and Africa, at shops, malls, bars, pubs, discos, in the street, in Church, at parties and live music gigs or "jumps" as they were called back in Nigeria.

Through it all though, despite his many failings, Peter heard the voices of family, sometimes distant, but always solid, refusing to be daunted, filling him with gratitude. Daily, as their voices crossed and re-crossed his brain, Peter realised how they had all changed with the years and away from common shores from each other, living British and Irish and Spanish and French and American and Austrian and Nigerian lives.

His sister Priscilla, who was based in California, was exceptionally good at calming his nerves when they were most fraught. His brothers Zik and Chu concentrated on practical stuff such as lawyers, accountants and media. Priscilla focused on the spirit. Peter was convinced that without her encouragement, the incorporeal part of him – his very soul -- might not have survived the experience of hell intact.

They were of course ordinary people, with faults and weaknesses and sometimes the pressure would get to everyone and a note of almost palpable disharmony would hang in the air like a dark cloud. But always they were shields against the forces of darkness that were threatening to destroy Peter.

Outside, the drizzle was becoming heavier, reminding Peter of England. *Oh for the delightfully eccentric sight of a plough team coming over the brow of a hill* – memories of the voice on BBC Radio 4, evoking images in Peter's mind of buggies drawn by Clydesdales and Shetland Ponies and picturesque little villages with thatched roofs along the Cornish coast in south west England – images that came back to him now as he thought of *old Blighty*. People would be relishing the few weeks in the summer when it actually got sunny and hot and the air was fresh and birds were singing and trilling away. Many Londoners would head for the seaside with their families, especially to areas around the county of Devon and

Cornwall. Places like Torquay, St Ives, Newquay and Penzance would be packed. People would hit the local pubs, turning the pavement into drinking pavilions, basking in the sunshine while he was in this dark cage of misery.

Meanwhile, the drizzle had turned into an angry storm, lashing the barred windows, lightning flashing across the skies, thunder barking angrily like all the hounds of hell had been let loose upon the earth. A huge scowling overhang of dark cumulus, matching Peter's mood perfectly. A great big black bear tumbling through the sky and blocking out the sun. A lightning flash, opening the heavens. The Yoruba Santerian god, Shango, racing across the sky aboard his chariot drawn by goats, swinging his invincible hammer, challenging the forces of evil, thunder roaring in his wake, the ever loyal Oshun by his side, on borrowed wings, swept by a powerful wind and a torrent of rain to the land of the giants, decreed by fate to keep the balance between good and evil.

Peter blinked! His mind was in turmoil. Was he becoming unhinged? He had to get some kip. He managed to close his eyes. There was that awful pounding, grinding, banging in his head again. A glass of water, some aspirin! That was the last thing he remembered before he fell into a troubled sleep.

6

"BED 88, BED 88, go to B stairwell. You have a professional visit."

The voice sounded harsh and aggressive. The whip crack in it startled Peter awake. With slightly unsteady legs, he made his way to the big red steel door that opened up onto the staircase. Down seven flights of spiral stairs. Peter found the descent highly unpleasant. He made his way through a narrow dimly lit corridor that twisted and turned like a maze, following the arrows on the wall.

A minute later, he turned a corner and the professional visiting room stood before him. It was about the size of a large queen size mattress and contained a desk, two chairs and a spy camera that bore down on the occupants from above, blinking obtrusively.

The lawyer was seated and he stood up when Peter entered the tiny room. After months of speaking to him on the phone from London and latterly from Atlanta, it was the first time Peter was setting eyes on him. And at such close proximity.

With a grotesquely sallow complexion, he looked like a walking cadaver. He had a bizarre tic on one side of his face. The other side was pock - marked. It had various craters, scarified hillocks and volcanoes -- like the terrain of the moon or a relief map of the rugged slopes of Afghanistan -- stretching from his temple down to his jaw line. Peter, his head foggy from sleep and fear, half-expected an exudation from one sorely pimpled fortification to turn into a sudden Taliban guerrilla charge upon him their besieger. He blinked to clear his head and the vision metamorphosed into stubble growing out of the rocks and stones on the cadavers face like saxifrage plants crowned with small dirty brown flowers.

The rest of the man's head looked like one of those cup-shaped receptacles used for transporting molten metal in a foundry. Peter noticed an enormous hooter sitting threateningly in the middle of the cadaver's pineapple face, like a long bracket cantilever projecting from a wall. It seemed to be set at a tilted angle and swung around dangerously whenever the cadaver moved his head, like a heavy cannon fixed only at one end. The other end rose up from just above his nostrils, like a tube of pasta stuffed with minced meat and vegetables. Peter had a sudden violent urge to give him a bloody nose. And afterwards, he thought spitefully, jeer at him and call him *fuck face*. He felt he had been betrayed, let down terribly by this very person who should have been his most trusted *paid* support.

The cadaver's handshake was wet and limp, like soft pulp. His responses were wooden and he seemed listless, pre-occupied with other thoughts. Spots of perspiration glistened on his brow. Peter tried and failed to disguise his contempt.

"I cant believe you fell for such an elementary trick", Peter spat out, his eyes cutting the cadaver to pieces, his anger simmering threateningly. "You should have known they were planning to arrest me. You should have informed me".

A small cut under the cadaver's hook - nose opened wide and became a mouth.

"It's gonna take a while to sort things out", the mouth said matter-of-factly, while the rest of the cadaverously stiff face it was attached to shifted slightly sideways to avoid eye contact. The voice sounded like the chanting of mendicant friars. "You're just gonna have to be patient".

Peter's heart hurried into palpitation. His body felt like a narrow tube in which hot liquid kept rising and depressing. Delicate ramified blood vessels, intervening between arteries and veins, making his head swim. Panic, smothering him, threatening to choke him and extinguish his soul like a candle.

"What do you mean by 'a while'?"

"Several weeks at least, maybe even months."

Oh God, no please! Not in here. Peter's voice – frantic, urgent!

"Months? I can't wait months. I simply wont make it. I've got to get out of here". *You don't understand. This is hell. I am living in hell.*

Pause! "Okay Peter. I'll try and get a reasonable bond during the arraignment Monday so we can get you atta here".

Insincere, ephemeral catchwords. How Peter hated the way this cadaverous American said *arraignment Monday,* dropping the *on* that in proper parlance rightfully belonged in the middle. Was there condescension in the man's voice? Amusement perhaps?

———

Back on the 7th floor, the meeting only served to deepen Peter's disquiet. The cadaver did not inspire the least bit of confidence and somehow talking to him, call it the prescience of someone in anguish, Peter knew without being told what the outcome of the arraignment would be. Judas had delivered his kiss of death. Not surprisingly, Peter's morale dipped dangerously.

Nevertheless, Peter clutched onto hope. He had to continue believing there was a way to get out of this mess, and that the arraignment and bond hearing would at least offer an opportunity. He had to see beyond the darkness, his brother Chu had said.

Peter had little choice but to submerge once again in that sea of delinquency and pray and wait for Monday to arrive. It needed almost inhuman patience and it tested him to the limit. Boredom and fear took turns eating away at his soul. He tried to cope by devouring every piece of reading material he could get his hands on. He wrapped himself in the enchantment of books, went *Through the Looking Glass*, reliving innocence lost via the rose-coloured world of *Alice in Wonderland*. Textbooks, magazines, novels! Heroes and villains! Cowboys and Indians! World events! The horrors of history! Unimaginable disasters!

In desperation he picked up his pen.

My Juliet

They have put me in jail, locked me away, but my soul has remained with you, my spirit that they cannot touch.   Heart of my heart, I come to you at the appointed time each day, laying my head on your breast, my thoughts becoming your thoughts, never going under, but rising like a phoenix.   I see you through the yellow haze of distant streetlights, the fog of dawn, the English rain, the rising sun. If I close my eyes, I can hear you breathe. In the world of the blind, I can feel you, the love of my life.   I open my eyes.   I am no longer by your side.   But I can see you in the distance.   I wave to you casually. You wave back uncertainly. Fog swallows you up.   I lose sight of you, but the smell, your fragrance, is strong.   I breathe deeply, closing out the sounds, caressing my body, my body that you have loved.   I turn full circle and I swear I can sense your face.   I hold onto its faint, muffled promise as I gently fall asleep.   In a few minutes, removed again from this criminal world, I will dream of you.   But for now... each of us...on our own...for a while.

Behind Peter in the viewing area, the TV was turned on full blast.

"Motherfucking ho", the voice slurred the words.

"Look at that sweet thang", said another, whistling.

"Heg! Heg! Heg!" cackled a third.

Peter wondered why the damn telly had to be turned up so loud.   Lovell his crack addict corner mate told him crack dealers were in the habit of doing business with the TV on at full volume.

"Crack cocaine has made the black community in America a jungle," he said, after a coughing fit. "The community used to be a garden but crack has made it a jungle. Now the jungle brings out the beast in us where the garden used to bring out the good in us. Jungle mentality is kill or be killed. Garden mentality is live and let live. We've become more motivated by crack and the money and power associated with it than the principles we have to live as a people. But now crack has whites more than us. Whites are using crack more than blacks but they have the resources not to go jail. I seen white millionaires who lost everything to crack. You listening to what I'm saying, killer?"

Peter said he was listening and for him to go ahead. Lovell paused and blew out his cheeks.

"The main thing crack does to the individual is it robs you of your will to do the right thing. To be clean, to lead a proper life. It robs you of who you are. You constantly seek it day to day. It becomes your world, your life, your job, your career, your education. I'm talking about addicts like myself. It becomes everything. You get up in the morning, you start looking for what's called an eye opener. If you're fortunate to have a few dollars you spend it on the eye opener. If you don't, you find somewhere to steal it. All day, you try to feed that addiction. Some spend fifty to five hundred dollars a day on it. Not one cent on food, clothes or housing! By 2am you've spent all your money on it so you have nothing to eat. You're sleepy but you have long since lost your home so you start sleeping in abandoned buildings and you don't wash and there's no change of clothes. That person was me. I could have put a down payment on an apartment, but all I did was buy crack. Most of these mo'fuckers in here are crack dealers or addicts. They are all addicted to something. If it ain't crack its something else. That's America today".

He was right about most of them -- black and white -- being addicted to something. There were crack addicts and powder cocaine addicts, heroin addicts and ecstasy addicts, marijuana, acid or speed addicts or combinations of two or three or all. And of course they were all addicted to cigarettes. You couldn't get any of the above legally in jail (although they were often brought in illegally), so they were all severely hooked on caffeine, the only legal drug that was available. People would race back to their lockers after meals to gulp down vats of strong black coffee. Those without would go around almost tearfully, pitifully begging for a cuppa.

One particular inmate, Steve, was the most wired individual Peter had ever met. He lived on strong black coffee, consuming a cup of the black stuff every 20 minutes or so. Most of the time, he walked around with his eyes wide open, as if he had a stick of dynamite up his arse.

It struck Peter that a significant number of lower class American youths were in deep trouble. Their minds were neglected and running wild. Many could hardly read or write. With little education and high addiction, what hope for a future?

7

DURING THE NEXT 48 hours, Peter attended Bible classes, met a variety of individuals and heard all kinds of shocking stories about glaring injustices and scandalous abuses. He also made his first acquaintances:

Greg, the excessively friendly Hillbilly with flaming red hair whom they nicknamed the birdman, because not only was he a bit of an odd bird in terms of his behaviour and the way he hopped about like a bird, he actually looked like he could have emerged from a hard-shelled egg. His face was disturbingly narrow, as if pressure had been applied at birth to the two sides of his head with such force, that it became squashed and deformed. His eyes seemed to be positioned around its corners and his beak of a nose was all the more prominent for it. He had reed thin arms and scaly legs and his body was covered with long red hair that could have passed for feathers -- all the parts rounded off with a large, protruding belly sitting near the base of an elongated torso.

The birdman had the annoying habit of turning up when you least wanted him to, fawning and grovelling for snacks. Once after a noisy breakfast, Peter lay down to read a book. The birdman suddenly appeared at his rack side. Peter knew why he was there. The previous day, someone had broken into his locker and stolen his provisions (or so he claimed, one could never be sure). Peter had offered him a pack of fruit cherries in sympathy. Since then, he began appearing at Peter's corner at regular intervals, especially during rest time when snacks were more likely to be eaten.

"Wanna play cards, Sir Peter?" he parroted.

Peter kept his eyes on the book. "No thanks mate".

He hovered for a moment, shifting his weight from one skinny leg to the other. Peter studiously ignored him, resisting the urge to scream at him to flap and fly away. He finally got the message and skipped away rather hastily.

There was Ngo, the Vietnamese pusher born in the communist north just before the bitter war against US-backed South Vietnam. Easily excitable and obsessed with having sex with virgins, he would describe one of his encounters in broken English, his tongue darting out with reptilian slick through a large gap where bottom front teeth should have been. Ngo had a great stock of jokes but very few could understand his English so he spent a lot of time on his own. It was his third run through jail. The first time he got ten years for killing a man. He claimed it was in self - defence but the court didn't believe him and banged him away for manslaughter. The other time and this time he was nailed for importing drugs and selling heroin from Thailand.

There was Vince, the handsome black former US army recruit, who served seven years in Germany and had six children by six different mothers.

"When I got out of the service, there was no job. One of my friends introduced me to cocaine and I started selling. I did what I had to do to maintain my harem", he says with a smirk. However, Vince had not been brought in for drugs, but for what he claimed was a trumped up charge of domestic violence by a girl he didn't want to be with.

"I went to a bar with her and I started dancing with another

girl. She gets mad and thinks I'm flirting. We go to her place
and I tell her I've had it with her. I leave and she calls the police
and tells them I threatened her. They arrest me on the way. I was
taken to court and asked to say something before my sentence. I
told the judge the system was corrupt and unfair and that I was
innocent. He got mad and gave me thirty days. I told him he
was conducting a kangaroo court and he gave me sixty days. I
told him to kiss my ass and he gave me ninety days. Look at me.
Ninety days of my life for a crime I didn't commit. The judge has
taken ninety days out of my life and he's getting paid for it".

And there was Cecil, a slightly older black army veteran of the
Vietnam war, who was a recovering crack addict.

"I became an addict because both Vietnam and America fucked
me up. I remember there were nine of us in Nam who went to
sleep as a group – four blacks and five whites. As we slept, all
the white guys had their throats cut. Their finger - nails and ear
- lobes were cut off and their weapons and dog tags taken. The
only thing they did to us black men was to take our weapons.
They left us a note: go home brother, we have no war with you.
Blacks were always put up front in that war. When we realised
we didn't mean anything to America and that we were being used
as fighting machines and the Viet Cong were fighting in self defence, the black man stopped fighting and America pulled out of
that war. As vets we feel slighted. Because of the shame of the
Vietnam War there was no welcoming parade. We are basically
the forgotten ones. No one marched for us, no one cared for us
and in some cases, even our families deserted us. Nobody cries
for us when we die".

After he was arrested for using crack, Cecil became deeply religious and often led the singing at church service on Sundays with
his resonant baritone.

There were Keith Abdul Kareem and Thomas X also known
as "Corky", both black Muslims. They had travelled to Africa
in October 1994, to attend the Nation of Islam's Saviour's Day
Convention in Accra, Ghana. Arguably, they were the only black

Americans in the entire jail to have travelled to the "motherland" and they found every opportunity to talk about it.

"That Convention was the greatest accomplishment of the Nation", Keith told Peter proudly. "Cos we brought nearly 2,000 black brothers and sisters from throughout the United States and the Caribbean to the African continent".

To which Thomas X, picking his teeth with a matchstick as if to deepen the significance of his words, added: "For most of them, it was the first time they put their foot on the African continent. Now I don't know about you, England, but I think that's important that they were able to see Africa and the African people not just as the projection of what's been on the media of starving babies with extended stomachs and flies all over them. But to know that there are societies in Africa and that people are living and functioning and trying to build their lives and that all the news from Africa is not negative".

There was Olu the Nigerian, who had tribal identification marks lashing his face, giving him a terribly aggressive look and earning him the nickname *Scar*face. He had been arrested for advance fee fraud or "419" as the Nigerians called it, after the section of Nigerian law that deals with such imposture. Apparently he and a few of his chums had conned some poor guy out of nearly three hundred thousand dollars, with promises of huge payments to come from some defunct Nigerian government account allegedly containing over 20 million dollars.

Back in Lagos Nigeria, Olu had been a money doubler, travelling through villages and towns, persuading people to part with their money and valuables, conning them into believing their investment would be doubled. With the arrival of the internet, Olu's trade moved up a notch, graduating from the street to the internet café and targeting the banks and the stock market, rather than the market stall owner and petty trader.

There was the Haitian Rasta, David, who with his amazingly thick dread locks, looked like branched antlers were growing out of his head. David would wake up every morning and yell: "Rise up brethren and prepare to chew the bread of sorrow". There would follow a series of incomprehensible rites and invocations -- apparently back in Haiti his father was a voodoo priest – aimed at affecting "black sorcery" (as one of the guards put it) and finding a magical solution to his current incarceration. David was also one hell of a singer and his voice, like the voice of one of those fabled Birds of Rhiannon in Celtic lore, would summon the deepest sentiments from inside Peter. David almost starved to death when he arrived on a domestic violence charge because he was vegetarian and they refused to make special provision for him. For a while, he lived on commissary donations from other inmates before the kitchen took pity on him.

There was of course Steve, the obsessive pseudo hillbilly from the Appalachian hills of Kentucky, mentioned earlier. They called him the "road runner" because he was always running up and down the hallway, excessive enthusiasm billowing from his wild eyes, wired out of his mind on black coffee, which as mentioned earlier, he drank steadily every 20 minutes. He was done for using crack. A notorious probation violator, he had been jailed several times before for the same offence. He was a borderline manic-depressive, which meant that he had disorderly, alternating periods of elation and depression. When he was up he was shooting through his head into the roof like Cheech and Chong going *Up in Smoke*. When he was languid low, it was of the self-destructive, suicidal kind. It took very little for him to swing either way, and when he was down everyone feared he might do something disastrously rash. For instance, when a money order from his brother did not arrive in time and he couldn't purchase snacks from the commissary -- which of course meant no coffee -- he sank into a very dark mood, moaning continuously and threatening to throw himself down seven flights of stairs. When it finally arrived, he was like a little child, full of joy, strutting the halls. He sat on his rack, cradling his provisions. He was king of the hills, lord of the rings, calling the shots again.

Everyone liked Steve because he was so child like. He looked forward to what most thought were extremely unimportant things -- like a kid at Christmas waiting for Santa Claus to come down the chimney. That's when he wasn't running around thinking he was Robert Shapiro, one of the lawyers on the OJ Simpson case. He was always reading the Revised Code and proclaiming that, "I ain't going to jail no more". Most people believed he lacked the will power not to violate his probation again.

There were the members of the Bible class: Anton and Darryl, Dan and Daniel, Winston the Liberian and Robert the anti-globalist.

At fifty, Winston was one of the oldest inmates on the 7th floor. His big round eyes were a little too close to his nose, giving him a stupid appearance. His face looked pained and lined with suffering, like a refugee on some forced extremely harsh, labour camp. He was originally from Liberia, a nation torn apart by years of civil war. Everyone thought he looked like Yoda from Star Wars, except his ears weren't as batty. But he had a most wonderful, kind and gentle soul and had somehow ended up at Queensgate, accused of not paying child support.

Another fellow that made Peter's acquaintance was Robert, a young, white middle class idealistic anti-globalist who bore a striking resemblance to Leonardo di Caprio. He was part of the multi-generation, multi-class group that led the anti WTO protests in Seattle. Although merely a small part of the anti-globalist movement, his zeal for a new world order was infectious and his middle class, educated background set him apart from the rabble. A youthful non-conformist, he was easily one of the most intelligent and philosophical characters at Queensgate and although he was nearly fifteen years younger than Peter, they instantly connected. They would sit up late into the night discussing third world debt and the new radicals. He was a combination of a dreamer and a subversive as well as an artist of extraordinary talent. He impressed Peter tremendously when, as if driven by unseen hands, he sculpted a most beautiful bible out of a bar of soap.

He had been caught with a small quantity of powder cocaine and sent to Queensgate for 180 days.

Of all the inmates he got to know, Peter became closest to Reid the Californian. As well as being about the same age, 39, they were both from out of state. He was the only other person in Peter's wing who had suffered the indignity of extradition under the most excruciating and humiliating circumstances. They both had the highest cash bonds. Part German and part Irish, he was also, like Peter, a Catholic by birth. Reid was no stranger to people of colour -- his stepfather and the man who brought him up from the age of four was Japanese. He was facing up to ten years in prison for drugs -- something he had inadvertently got into by naively agreeing to post a quantity of narcotics from California to a distant relative in Ohio.

Reid was easy to get along with. In less than an hour he and Peter were chatting and laughing like old friends. Reid's biggest fear was that he would miss seeing his six-year old son grow up.

"How are you supposed to teach your children to take pride in your country when you know the country is simply taking a large dump on you? Look at me! First time offender. The country is planning to lock me up for ten years because I don't have any money. I'll miss the chance to see my kid grow up. All I can stand to be away from him is at the most four years. But they're planning to put me away for ten years. They might as well shoot me. No wonder there's such a high suicide rate in America. I wonder why the psychologists and all the head people cant see the problem. America has become a melting pot of insanity".

Reid became like a brother to Peter and their friendship made moments of desperate sadness seem less severe. He had a tremendously hearty American sense of humour and being from California added a touch of light-hearted irreverence to many things. He had an impressive reserve of mirth even when things seemed very bleak. During those times, they seemed beyond danger, beyond the capriciousness of their persecutors.

Reid also had a quite alert mind -- a rare commodity in that environment. They had endless theological and philosophical discussions about everything from the Bible to astronomy. Peter remembered those times vividly and with great affection.

Peter probably would have had a more difficult time, might not have made it with his mind and body intact, if it hadn't been for Reid's presence. In addition to the humour and intellectual stimulation, Reid was a big guy, over six feet and weighing in at about 260 pounds. He was a former amateur boxer and with his considerable size helped to keep some of Peter's tormentors at bay.

By the time Peter left Reid had added a large bit of extra weight. Much of his muscle had turned into fat and he reminded Peter of a mound of pounded yams. He would reach into his locker with a plump hand and grab a honey bun, regarding it thoughtfully before conveying it to his capacious mouth. He would take a swig of hot chocolate, heave a fat sigh and settle down to talk.

"I wonder what my purpose is here", he would say with a grimace, his sad hooded hazel eyes looking like pools of stagnant water. "I am yet to discover. I see a ray of light, a twinkle of sunlight in my eye. I think this is it, my chance for freedom. Only to hear a phone call from the lawyer and it's back into that tunnel of darkness again. Back to wondering what is my purpose? What does God want me to do here? I still haven't received an answer. It's so lonely waiting for this answer. Only someone in this situation would understand. I feel damned, like that character in *A Christmas Carol*, Ebenezer Scrooge's partner, Marley, with coils of chains around him. Only I don't feel I forged those chains in life because I am not a bad man. Now I know how the slaves felt in chains. All I have is my mind. Sometimes I wonder if I can keep a hold of it or if it's slipping off too."

They had all been thrown together by some unseen impetus that coerced and compelled them and for several months they shared the same world, praying and laughing and crying together, lifting and supporting one another.

Because of Peter's British background, the detainees truly de-

lighted in talking with him a "real live black Englishman", as one
of them put it. Never mind that he tried repeatedly to tell them
he was British African, not English. Peter suspected that engag-
ing him in discourse made some of them who had never travelled
out of their neighbourhoods, not to mention their country, feel
socially mobile. Here they were from the inner cities of America
and suddenly breathing the same air as this most exotic creature
with "that accent", like something from "tee vee", as indeed he
was.

Everyone gave him a nickname. The blacks called him
"England" and the whites named him "Sir Peter". Robert would
joke and say: "Arise Sir Peter, and pack your shit", amid much
laughter. Sometimes when he blew his nose, which in that air-
conditioned environment and with the state of his sinuses was
quite often, someone would quip: "England's blowing his brains
out again."

8

3.00AM. WAKE UP CALL. Court Day.

The voice of the guard in his sleepy ear was like the crack of a whip.

"All courts get up, wash your face, brush your teeth, line up at B stairwell and spread 'em. Remember you cant take nuthin' with you, just your court papers. No candy, no tissue, no pencils, just your court papers".

A few grumbled and moaned but Peter and nineteen other detainees dutifully trooped to the big red door for the first series of frisks. Down seven flights of stairs to the "chow hall" for breakfast. Afterwards, frisked again, then handcuffed. In and out of a series of cages -- *Ling Ling* the Panda on transfer from one zoo to another: the holding cage in admissions, the mobile cage for the drive to the Justice Centre, the lift cage to the 6th floor, the exit cage. Handcuffs removed. Wait for three hours doing nothing, listening to bleary-eyed inmates filling the enclosed space with groaning yawns and smelly farts. Then finally to the court holding cage or "bull pen" for another four-hour wait, sitting on uncomfortably hard, cold steel benches.

Around 11am, Peter was ordered out of the holding cage and step hustled down a flight of stairs and a long dark corridor by two beefy CO's. They paused for a few moments outside a heavy door. One of the CO's moved aside and whispered conspiratorially into a walkie - talkie. Peter blinked nervously. It seemed his entrance was being timed to be an event. It was.

Minutes later, *like a condemned man to the scourging, the patibulum bearing down on his flagellated shoulders,* Peter was led in chains to the courtroom and his undoing.

The *mise en scene* was nothing short of pure theatre, show time American style and what a show. The media had waited patiently, now they closed in. Cameras rolled and lights flashed. Photographers and notepad clutching journos rushed forward, prosecutors stood up and fiddled with their neckties - strips of brightly coloured cloth with which Peter would have dearly liked to choke the lot.

Peter couldn't believe it. A serial killer could not have expected a more dramatic reception. The press had come to turn their own into Ohio's biggest rogue. Peter was guilty even before the arraignment took place. He had become a veritable banquet for them. And now they were ravenously consuming his grief and humiliation with open delight, devouring his brave, desperate, pathetic attempts to hold his head up high. There was no place to hide from the scrutiny of mocking, dismayed and pitying eyes. Everywhere Peter looked, there was someone who knew him. He could not lose himself in nameless crowds. There was nowhere he could go to be alone.

Peter stood there, dazed by a formidable arsenal of flashing lights, a low dull sound like a blow growing into huge rapid thuds of palpitation like galloping dinosaurs, erupting in his chest. A loud rumbling crashing noise exploding in his head. More lights flashing, his mouth and throat instantly dry. Buried by his comrades, the media. The very institution that had built him up was now his undoing, the source of his misery. All his hard work made so pointless by them.

Wait a minute, Peter thought. *That's ME in handcuffs, on camera!* A monstrous, grotesque, perverse, sickening, frightening nightmare! The lens trained on him, watching him. A fiendish presence, staring him in the eyes, taking its time in tormenting him, relishing his fear and pain, then closing in and exhausting his contents, feasting upon him greedily, sucking him into its hideous belly.

As Peter was being paraded in handcuffs in front of the press, the judge made his grand entrance. One sympathetic corrections officer asked the chief prosecutor whether he should take the cuffs on Peter's hands off.

"No", he barked.

His eyes cold as ice rested on Peter briefly before quickly darting away. Serpent! This was his trial of the century. The most he could hope for in his provincial world. He had prepared for this performance and now he readied for take off. Peter could see the immense thrill of power on his face as the flashlights exploded and the cameras rolled.

"A British Nigerian…hiding in England and west Africa…an international news correspondent…earning over $200,000 a year…thumbing his nose at the American justice system…a fugitive from US law…we ask your honour to set bail at $145,000 times 10…"

Peter looked stricken. He could not believe what he was hearing about himself. He felt dizzy. A hissing sound like steam from a whistling kettle rushed through his head, threatening to drown him. This could not possibly be planet earth. He had heard that prosecutors were generally publicity mad, but this one stood out among his peers. Peter was at once appalled and fascinated by the man's ambitious drive for publicity. Incredulous that he could sensationalise this case in order to make it seem more important. Such…such…mendacity! They must all know he certainly didn't deserve to be labelled as a criminal. But elections were coming up and if that's what it took to get their names and faces on TV, then so be it. Such, such…rampant ambition!

Peter's chest welled with passion. He had an overpowering need to defend his honour.

"Can I say something?"

"No", said the judge coldly, "speak through your lawyer".

His lawyer, the cadaverous mute. His erstwhile shield bearer, *paid* defender, shepherd, torch out of darkness, suddenly turned wimp, barely summoning up the weakest defence, making a feeble attempt, handing over tax papers, letters from the BBC.

"Your honour, the defendant is putting up $11,000 and his brother is talking about putting up his house… I've got to get details of that…" Wank, wank, wank, went the wanker! Unable to explain the concept of the British Inland Revenue…And this was the man on whose shoulders his fate rested…so miserably inadequate, so pitifully unable to comprehend a wider world. What a bloody bunch of jokers, thought Peter angrily. The worst part of it was they didn't know it. On the contrary, they thought somehow the rest of the world did nothing but dream about their frigging country.

Why hadn't that cadaverous twit mentioned the deal he'd made with them, the one about Peter coming voluntarily and guaranteeing he would not be arrested? Unless of course he was in on it… Betrayer! A highly publicised arrest and now this…humiliation!

The final act in the show! As Peter looked on in anaphylactic shock, the chief prosecutor put on his most warlike attitude. He snarled with animal truculence at the British Nigerian. Then baring his teeth, he growled pugnaciously at the cameras, once again demanding his pound of flesh:

" …A foreigner…a flight risk…no extradition treaty with England…let him go and you won't see him again…the state of Ohio DEMANDS THAT YOU SET BOND AT $145,000 TIMES 10".

The prosecutors' voice, chilling, rose when he uttered his last sentence, forcing Peter to recoil. He felt as if molten lava was rushing through his skull.

The judge said: "Let's not get carried away now. Bond is set at $180,000 cash". And he slammed down his gavel. That was it. The decision was as unchangeable as stone. *Thanks a lot judge. Now all I have to do is go to my account and pull out $180,000 in cash and I'd be a free man.*

An exultant smile from the prosecutor. A sudden movement of the head crowned in unassailable glory. What was that? Did that bastard just nod and wink at me, Peter in his misery, wondered? It was only there for the tiniest moment, then it was gone. But the message was loud and clear. *We got you where we want you now sucker! Banged up at our pleasure.*

Peter's head boiled. It was clear the direction of this particular hearing had been decided even before he stepped into court. A staged arraignment, for the benefit of the cameras! They probably knew he wouldn't flee, but they asked for it anyway. It quickly dawned on Peter that with a bond that high – and they wanted raw cash -- he was stuck in their custody. The only way he was getting out was to be found not guilty.

Peter's head raged. Every step of the way he had followed the prescription of lawyers, even agreeing to come voluntarily. Yet they had conspired to destroy him. Shocking! Creatures without conscience! Legal hooligans! His lawyer, the cadaver, in whom he had placed his trust, who had given his word, powerless in the face of them!

As Peter was led away weak and dejected following his excoriation, trailed by a horde of reporters, cameras and microphones, a kindly voice:

"Mr Oti". Peter looked back.

"Nick Botsford, Channel 5 News. I'd very much like to hear your side of the story. Would you care to speak to me sometime?" He sounded sincere. Peter filed his name away in his mind.

"I am innocent and this whole thing is a charade".

Peter walked away or rather allowed himself to be forcibly led away.

Dear Jul, I searched the hallway and saw your face. Do not forget me. Pray for me. Hold me in your heart as I hold you. Courage, you smiled. I smiled back. Then you vanished. I could not be sure it had happened.

It was without doubt the worst and most humiliating hour of Peter's entire life. He felt isolated, afraid and alone, in a strange, barbaric country. The condemned heretic, awaiting with fearful anticipation, his roasting at the stake.

Sitting with his lawyer the cadaver afterwards, watching his disreputably shifty eyes, mottled face and that detestable tic, Peter felt a deep abominate loathing for him. How could he have trusted this simpleton, this...corpse, this legal lowlife, this disgusting, offensive, repulsive, hatred–arousing, small time punk who had the gall to demand more money? Peter made up his mind he was going to fire him.

"Just what the hell happened here?" Peter spat, hardly able to contain his anger.

The lawyer's treacherous eyes wouldn't meet his.

"I told you these people were devils", was all he could say through ranks of gapless, serrated teeth.

"It's got nothing to do with them and everything to do with you. You didn't deliver again. Every step of the way, you have failed to deliver. You assured me you'd made a deal and that deal wasn't honoured. Then you promised to arrange a reasonable bail and again, nothing. You weren't even in court to talk to me. You turned up thirty seconds before the judge in your sharp new suit. All of you, using my misfortune to get your faces on TV and further your careers".

With a huge effort Peter restrained his anger, knowing he was all there was going at the moment, badly wanting to scream some more at him, biting his tongue.

Half an hour later, back to the holding cage. Inmates returning from various courtrooms after sentencing, continuance, bond setting, arraignment, plea or trial! No dismissals or acquittals! That's the way it was in Ham County.

3.00pm. End of court day! Of the twenty from Queensgate who went before judges, five had been sent away to penitentiaries up state.   Peter and the rest of the collection of wild animals in captivity headed back.   It was the same process again for the return journey -- cage after cage -- a blur of cages -- till they reached the admissions cage.

Peter was on the verge of starvation.   They had not eaten anything since breakfast at 5am.   They were given cold, stale bologna sandwiches and a syrupy orange drink for lunch.   Peter tried to bring it to his mouth but his hands were shaking so badly he promptly put the sandwich down. *He who had held court with presidents and the Pope, been in and out of the White House and Downing Street, inspired people with a few well chosen words on the global news networks – BBC, ITN, SKY, CNN -- now reduced to this, an inmate in chains with shaking hands...*

Peter looked around to see if anyone was watching and sure enough a number of them were.   One who had the sleepy eyes of a newt and a sly unctuous grin said with mock sympathy.

"Nigger, you really stressed out, ain't you?"

Nigger! American blacks on the streets called themselves "niggers", the very word that had been used against them during slavery and segregation, a perjorative term that labelled them as less than human and was used to justify some of the inhuman treatment they received. The word was now being used by poor blacks to describe themselves -- a sort of brotherhood of the streets.   Whites were of course not allowed into this brotherhood and their use of the term in reference to a black man was seen in a most negative light.   If you were white and used the term, better be ready for a rough fight -- and in the case of jail where blacks are the overwhelming majority, a severe beating with potentially fatal consequences. On this they were indivisible. You say that to a black guy and the pit bull bitch comes out in him.

Peter waited for a few minutes, then tried again. Success! He wolfed down the sandwich before returning to the sleeping cage that was home.

9

ALONE! AFRAID! DESPONDENT! DESPERATE!
Dear Juliet

I am keeping myself strong but as for not letting my thoughts be troubled, that is not easy. I am restless and discontented, un-reconciled to the present state of things, living in unimaginable pain, like someone pierced my side with a spear, lanced my soul, grievously wounding my spirit. The terrible realisation that I am inescapably mired in the thick of it is slowly, painfully dawning on me. I have tumbled into a world of strident fascism and I have to somehow hold the ring. I feel as if my head is about to explode…my head that has turned into a football and is being kicked around in this political game, the sport of the persecutors…

Peter felt an overpowering urge to breakdown and weep, but he knew he couldn't cry here in this jail and certainly not at this waking hour when the mean hearted could pounce on it as a sign of weakness. But he could at least cry out in his soul. He wanted *Chicken Licken's* sky to fall and close over his head, protecting him from the venom of those who wanted to hurt him.

Peter had a horrible fear that after his impossibly high bond was set the interest of his relatives in him would wane, decreasing in vigour and importance until it died off. Not because they didn't care, but because no one could afford such a bond and that somehow it had magnified and exaggerated his reason for being arrested in the first place.

The perspective was clear. To the prosecutors...*persecutors!!!...* distended with grand, puffed up, bombastic ambition, he was nothing more than ego fodder, to be used to con the masses and deliver the vote that would keep them in power so they could continue to leap down on the people from a worryingly great height.

Peter now had it. The so-called epistemological privilege! That elusive term introduced by liberationists to describe how people on the lowest rungs of society had the benefit of seeing the true structure and injustice of things because they bore the full weight of it. From the bottom up! The fat cats sitting on them, squashing them, suffocating them, farting and pissing and shitting on their upturned faces. A theory of liberation knowledge, now unequivocally validated!

Peter was no longer fully connected to the world of flesh and blood. Only, here and there, episodically, at sequenced intervals, like some weekly TV sitcom, each one distinct but part of the whole. He felt like a contrivance originated by people convulsing and quivering with pleasure and lust. A soulless, expurgated worthless husk, empty from the inside.

Peter's movements were no longer fluid, but marked time with a regular tic and a jerky spastic motion, like a robot or a breakdancer. He was no longer the whole that consisted of parts, but a thousand fragments, broken to pieces. Stuck in an extremely narrow dark tunnel, head drooping, wearily, utterly spent!

Peter needed to talk to someone, anyone who would listen. His whole being craved sympathy, a nod of understanding, pity from others. But none was to be found. He tried to take his mind off himself, away from the fear and worry and despair. He tried to read, to think, but every attempt only deepened his anxiety and claustrophobia.

From somewhere back there, a vacantly silly, disembodied voice.

"Hey England, you on TV men!"

Peter ignored the voice and pulled the sheets tightly over his head.

The newspapers and the evening news! Dissimulating hypocrites! Sultans of Spin! Pretentiously postulating moral standards to which their own behaviour did not conform. Setting him up, leaping down on him from a dizzyingly great height. Gushing promiscuously, in a lustful, effusive, copious stream. Battling to out do one another in demonising of him. Twisting and twirling and twining and rotating and wrenching and distorting and interweaving, until lies seemed like the truth. *Former BBC correspondent... CNN anchor...International reporter...Earning over $200,000 a year... Callous, pitiless, uncaring father of a young American child... Whose hardworking mother had to go on welfare because this heartless monster... This king of the deadbeats...could not find it in him to send even a penny to help...*

Peter dozed off fitfully. He was immediately gripped by the most grotesque, vivid and disturbing nightmare. He dreamt he was back in feudalistic times. Vassals held land from their superiors in exchange for allegiance and service. Payment was in kind or by barter. Violence ruled! Might was right. The powerful dominated the weak. Only the fittest survived. Man and beast ran side by side on dusty by ways. Cincinnati had become a medieval town with a medieval court system, somewhere lost in time. Peter could see skeletons on the road, buzzards flying overhead, some guy in a witches outfit, dungeons with torches lit on the wall, black cats following him around. Suddenly the guy in the witches outfit was towering over him and repeatedly saying:

"Lock his arms...chain his feet...tie a stone to his leg...if he sinks he's guilty, if he floats he's innocent..."

Peter opened his eyes. Early morning. Those damn lights and awful thundering loudspeakers again. He had been sleeping since early evening. With great reluctance, he peered out from under the sheets. People were shuffling back and forth, to and from the bathroom.

He felt for his shoes but couldn't find them. He leaned over the edge of his rack to where they normally stood but they were not there.

Peter was not amused. He regarded passing inmates suspiciously. What the hell does someone want with shoes that had no shoelaces?

Peter looked down again. The shoes had not reappeared. It was indisputable. They had vanished.

Peter turned to Lovell, his corner mate.

"Have you seen my shoes?"

Lovell paused, turning the question over in his sluggish mind. Then he said slowly. "Dem guys took your shoes, man. Dey say you de worst dead beat dad in Ham County".

Peter stiffened.

"What guys?" he asked, looking around uneasily.

The crack addict stared at Peter. An overcast cumulus formation passed over his face. His voice was sharp with edge.

"Ya don' 'xpec me to snitch on 'em, do ya?" And he walked away.

Peter sat up. The warning device inside him was transmitting strong signals. His head was ringing, his nostrils flared, aroused by a sharp sense of danger. He broke out in a sweat, in spite of the arctic air conditioning. Cold blood charged up his spine, threatening to rush into his throat and annihilate him.

Peter stood up. There was that dreadful ringing in his head again. Alarm! Fear! Frightened expectation of unimaginable difficulty!

It dawned on him that the previous night, whilst he was asleep and enduring a series of terrifying nightmares, the *rabble* had been avidly watching reruns of his arraignment and bond hearing on television late into the night. By morning, most inmates would have seen him and his sack of dirty laundry on TV. Here the box rules.

The shock of this new and threatening reality hit Peter and he found his legs were unsteady. He sat down abruptly, like a stricken bull. A sick, sinking feeling washed over him in waves. Play it cool, Peter told himself. These guys were dangerous.

As casually as he could, Peter got up, put on his standard issue slippers and headed for the bathroom.

Stares! Eyes wide with curiosity, surprise, admiration, bewilderment, horror and contempt. Open-mouthed, unpleasantly prominent stares! *Striking* stares, *thrusting* stares, staring him insane. Reducing him to rubble with their unrelenting insolence. Not like Britain where it is considered rude to gawk. More like Nigeria where people gape. Peter could feel himself flagging and wilting under the heat of their withering gaze.

Suddenly, the Tannoy crackled loudly.

"Okay folks this is your early morning wake up joke. Today is National Deadbeat Day. Fuck the kids!"

A hideously insensitive comment coming from the duty Corrections Officer, aimed with deadly accuracy at Peter. His idea of a joke! *The one who is supposed to protect me, erecting obstacles in my path! Agent provocateur! Inciting the mob of angry men, the people from nowhere, with nowhere to go, minds shredded, baying for my blood, assaulting me with their anger and frustrations.*

The CO's words were greeted with much hooting and laughter. It was just what the bullies need.

The *crime boss*, whom Peter christened Biter, loved it. He was Puerto Rican with a mix of African American and Amerindian blood. He had amazingly long, wiry arms, like a tree-living Sumatran anthropoid ape – *Pongo Pygmaeus* catching butterflies -- with even longer, needle thin, hairy legs growing out of a short trunk. At 45, he was an ageless *enfant terrible,* an indiscreet and unruly gang leader who controlled a group of inmates. His numerous arrests were tattooed onto his arms. The latest, C.C.W. -- carrying a concealed weapon -- was written in stovetop black ink across his mocha coloured forearm. His long hair was braided, pulled back tightly into a ponytail, exposing high cheekbones on a scraggy face, pencil thin beard and vicious reptilian eyes. An apparition from hell!

Biter's rack was on Peter's way to the bathroom. He and three others were looking at a newspaper as Peter attempted to walk past.

"Hey", Biter said, holding up the newspaper. "Ain't this you?"

Peter looked at the page and sure enough there was his picture next to the headline.

Biter's voice was full of accusation.

"It's you ain't it? Deadbeat motherfucker! You African mo' fuckers with your English accents coming here to hurt our American women. I bet you got $250,000 in the bank cos you a tee vee anchorman and you don't wanna pay. I atta hit you upside yo' head, deadbeat motherfucker".

Red, hot hate, burning like charcoal embers in his eyes. A few others came over to get front row seats. Peter ransacked his brain, searching for something that would appease him.

"Let me tell you what happened", Peter said nervously. "It's all lies".

It was hopeless. Biter had found his victim and he had a waiting audience to entertain. He was standing up shaking his fist.

"We don' wanna hear your bullshit, motherfucker. You the biggest deadbeat mo'fucker in America. That's what the tee vee say and the tee vee don' lie".

Bastard! Cheeky street punk! Shouts of approval from the crowd, spurring him on! He revelled in it. There's no stopping him now.

"I'm 'o kick yo' British ass. You in New Jack City now! This is America, killer".

More hecklers joined in. It was getting progressively dangerous. Someone started to chant: "Dead beat dad! Dead beat motherfucking dad!" The crowd swelled. Some started to clap in time with the chanting. Others made ugly faces and noises. They booed, they shouted, they laughed, they barked. Peter feared for the worst.

Then the loudspeaker crackled.

"Genlmen, chow time. Chow time! Go to B stairwell immediately. Repeat, immediately! Its chow time".

Peter was so grateful to that loudspeaker he started to shake. As casually as he could, he walked away. He was safe for now but he could feel their eyes on his back, taking aim, opening fire.

Later that morning as Peter walked into the refectory a sea of eyes followed his every step. Hushed whispers rustled through the hall like wind through dry leaves. He could hear snatches of them. *That's England...he's fucked...how the hell did he get in here from London...he ain't from London, he from Avondale...ain't no niggers come from London...sure they do, I seen that nigger Lenny Henry on tee vee and that heavy weight boxer Lennox Lewis with the drea'locks...*

Peter felt intensely curious eyes drilling holes in his back, burning into his hide like a welding torch. Some were sympathetic eyes. Others were like darts shooting hate into him.

Shortly after the incident with Biter, Peter made an appointment to complain to the social worker, a handsome, middle-aged mixed race woman, with enormous breasts called Jackie Pryor. She smiled what seemed like the most marvellous smile Peter, in the prime of his deprivation, had ever seen. A warm dimpled, *lustful?* smile. Peter's eyes stole down her neck...*my, what huge melons... what magnificent formations you've got there...got to be a bra busting 36D at least.*

The proud owner of those things -- those heavy baps Peter badly wanted to touch -- showed him into her office, bending over him to explain the complicated complaints form, looking deep into his eyes – such warmth! *Errant thoughts, scampering through his mind* – would it, could it be possible – in here? – And why did she remain bent over like that…her face next to his -- inches away, intoxicating him with that perfume, smiling libidinously. Peter felt himself ignite with desire.

"There's not much to it really", she was saying brightly, describing the complaints form, her face…inches away…such kissable lips…wondrous eyes…

Peter found his eyes drawn to those enormous mamms again. He had a sudden irresistible urge to dive into her bosom and stay there all day, playing with them. *It would be nice wouldn't it? Stick one on either side of his face, wobble them vigorously*…comical, wasn't it, how a pair of those things could lay hold of a man, especially one who's locked away. *Control yourself! Practice restraint! After all, they are just mounds of fat*…Christ, that plunging neckline! He could see part of a broad ring of colour coming through just above the frills of her dress. If those were her areolas, looking like halos, how big and pointy would her nipples be, especially when erect? Oh God! Had he been staring? It was supposed to be a quick, subtle glance – whoops! Not quite quick enough! *You're nicked, mate!*

"Fill in all the blank spaces and," – she gave him a sympathetic knowing smile and said in a low confidential voice "I'm not supposed to, but I'll make us some coffee and you can tell me all about England and the Queen…"

Knock! Knock! Knock! A CO knocking on the door shook Peter violently out of his reverie. "Gotta take him up Miss Pryor. Count time!"

Peter was speechless with disappointment. He shook his head as the CO pulled him by the arm. He lifted his hands, suddenly aware that she had noticed how weak and under *their* control he was. Such utter powerlessness! She gave him a pitying smile. But it was hopeless. He knew the moment was gone. So he thanked her and left.

Back on his rack, Peter buried his face in his hands. He must have been nuts to have thought that anything could have happened down there. No matter what he was on the outside, inside he was a prisoner. *Their* prisoner! Nothing more, nothing less! He simply could not imagine her having it off with him.

A sudden wave of guilt and shame washed over him as he thought of Juliet. What a disgraceful, totally inexcusable act of disloyalty to have even considered such a thing. How could he have looked her in the face if something had happened?

His severely deprived penis might of course have had other plans, just like it did at University when he found himself, despite his relationship with a Caribbean model, obliging that crazy bald headed chick with the ill-favoured face and athletic body from Kenya, who invited him over to help with her English history revision, with particular focus on the rights and legal procedures enshrined in the Magna Carta, which she found confusing.

But instead of revision, she suddenly starts giggling and pouring honey all over her head, letting it run down past her breasts. And Peter didn't need a second invitation and was on those tits like a hawk, licking away, before she went on her knees and poured honey all over his member and blew him till he thought he would faint. Then he flipped her over and cock punched her while she screamed with pleasure. And there had been many others since those school days, hadn't there?

Peter lay on his rack fantasising, guilt suspended for the moment, replaced by rampant lust. He imagined being with each one of them all over again. Then he imagined banging them three at a time. Then the guilt returned with a vengeance.

Jackie Pryor kept her promise though and sent for him several times but all they ever did was talk. Peter was still amazed by the size and quality and comeliness of her cleavage but he had learned to practice restraint and somehow managed to keep his eyes on her face. She was terribly simple-minded but with a heart of pure gold. She was sympathetic and seemed quite taken by Peter. He suspected he was a novelty, a breath of fresh air in her otherwise dreary life. She took to inviting him down to her neat and relatively spacious office to give him a break from the suffocating feeling of the cage. She talked intimately to him about her life, especially her two failed marriages.

Peter liked her and didn't mind her telling him about herself. Even when he grew tired of her tales of woeful love, he encouraged her by looking intensely interested. He feared that if he left her office, his life would fall back into the emptiness and despair of jail. So he let her prattle on. Eventually he would return to the cage and for the rest of the day would read voraciously some of the books she had loaned to him.

During those long days and nights in captivity and in between court appearances, Peter consumed everything he could lay his hands on with a passionate fire. What else could he do under the circumstances?

He read the Bible from cover to cover, rediscovering parts he had long forgotten. Fascinating stories about the terrible wrath of God and some quite extraordinary characters: Jacob and Esau, David and Goliath, David and Saul, Samuel, Solomon, Nebuchadnezzer, Daniel, Shadrack, Mishak and Abednego, Saul who became Paul. He pored over the Revised Code -- a very big law book several hundred pages long, full of American legalese. *A book about how I'm gon' keep you locked down!*

At night, he wept copiously under his blanket.

"God, my only refuge", he cried into his pillow. "Help of the helpless, do not leave me now". Somehow he had to find the faith from deep inside him to believe that in spite of the long, dark night, dawn would eventually come.

In the morning, Peter awakened to the sound of that obtrusive Tannoy crackling into life and that hideously thick southern American drawl.

"Genlmen, wake up...git up off of your racks, make your beds, we're next for chow..."

Peter pulled the sheets over his head but could not evade that eerie light, that guttural voice.

10

WHENEVER THE DETAINEES CAME together in forced congregation -- eating, social welfare, court, outside recreation -- Peter
tried not to speak and to blend in. He avoided eye contact. If he
looked at them, it happened when their attention was focused on
something else. He would watch unseen, perversely anonymous,
eyes hooded, assigning marks, separating them according to their
behaviour, condemning his tormentors to anguish and suffering.

Invariably someone would say something to him and he
would be forced to respond. Immediately, his accent would set
him apart and he would be recognised as the "guy on tee vee" and
in the papers. Some were friendly and others fascinated. Some
poked fun at him and others instantly hated his guts.

With a masters degree and years of experience as a television reporter and presenter Peter was better educated and more exposed
than any other detainee in the building. It was something that
earned respect and resentment in almost equal measure, as much
from the inmates as the guards. Many of them did not go beyond
high school. Peter discovered to his amazement that quite a few

CO's and inmates alike could hardly read or write and certainly couldn't spell many simple words. They would come up to him and ask how to spell words like "knee, lying, plea" etc. Peter often helped the Corrections Officers to draft letters and the inmates to prepare their court statements.

With "that accent" Peter was expected to know everything and compared to them he did. Many of them felt awed, intimidated or downright resentful whenever they were around him. Some of them in deference wouldn't look at him directly when they spoke to him. Others took an instant dislike to him, detecting unruffled arrogance in all his utterances and truth be told, Peter did sometimes employ the characteristic British double speak when talking to some of them. They were never quite sure whether they were being complimented or insulted and that offended their simple straight - forward American approach in no small measure.

11

Commissary Day!

Larcenous rogues and villains, meandering in and out of the shadows, unable to resist the temptation to plunder on this day when inmates who could afford to were allowed to spend money at the commissariat, stocking up on provisions and rare delicacies like chocolate, biscuits, fruit drinks, crisps (chips for the Americans), snacks and writing materials. Their compulsive need to steal other people's "booty" was written in their eyes and movements and as commissary hour approached a strong sense of kleptomania pervaded the air. Pirate inmates lurked in the shadows, sniffing the air predaceously, searching out the most vulnerable -- first timers, bewildered foreigners, middle class whites. They would choose the moment after the victim returned from the commissariat to turn up at his rack to grovel for something -- body lotion, pencil or some such. As the unsuspecting first-timer opened his locker wide to search for whatever had been begged for, the plunderers would observe the contents, wait for him to go to the showers or use the lavatory, then strike. After clearing its contents, they moved on to the next locker and victim. Nothing happened to them because no one was ever prepared to live with the consequences of breaking the code of silence – "snitching" as it was called.

Peter fell victim to these unscrupulous elements after his first commissary visit.   He had gone to the play area for a chat and a game of American checkers with Olu the Nigerian.   The game had taken longer than usual because Olu was peppering Peter with questions about Nigerians living in Britain, having never been to the UK himself and Peter had to take time off the game to answer them. Peter was not particularly fond of Olu, but merely tolerated him. Olu was quick-tempered and as fierce as the ethnic marks on his face made him look.   Facing Peter, he shouted questions at him in an accent thick with the odd rhythmic phonetic habits of the *Yoruba*, which he had carried over to his English, where words such as "how, hair, hand" came out as "ow, air, and".

"I ear dat deer ah so many Nigerians living in London, dey are calling it "Little Lagos", Olu yelled into Peter's face, forcing him to jerk back his head in alarm.

Involuntarily, Peter found himself shouting back the answer. "Yes that's absolutely right. London and in particular one of its southern boroughs known as Peckham has possibly the largest overseas Nigerian community in the world, with around 40% of Peckham's population born in Nigeria or in the UK of Nigerian descent.   The vast majority are of Yoruba or Igbo extraction. Nigerians have actually been living in London since the 18th Century, mostly those who were part of the slave trade. Between 1967 and 1970, quite a few refugees fleeing from the Nigerian civil war settled in the UK. But the more recent wave started arriving from the mid 80's".

When Peter eventually returned to his corner, he found his locker hanging half open. Its contents or what was left over -- essentially personal items like socks and underwear -- were scattered carelessly about the floor. The "goodies" were all gone, about twenty-five dollars worth, a heck of a lot in jail terms. Peter never found out who did it because nobody was prepared to speak out.

Later that day, the anti-globalist Robert also had his locker raided in an organised hit. Peter actually observed the two blokes who did it, saw them casing Robert's corner during a basketball game on television that had everyone's attention diverted. Peter told Robert what he had seen but Robert resolutely refused to report it. He would not snitch on other inmates because he feared the consequences. This of course meant that the thieves were walking around freely and as such remained a clear and constant threat. Robert was probably wise not to report them. They were part of the gang controlled by Biter the crime boss and they would not have hesitated to punish him severely.

There were at least two different black gangs operating at Queensgate. They were from different "hoods" and congregated in their own designated areas. Sometimes they crossed each other and had to be separated forcibly by a rush of guards. They moved around in groups, each gang using their own slang words, their own sing song voice -- even their own laugh -- sounding terribly alike. It was often difficult for Peter to figure out which one had spoken.

While in jail, most would never openly admit to being gang members because the authorities frowned on it. But all you had to do was look at the tattoos that served as their identification marks. They also had certain handshakes that members of their particular gang could recognise.

"This ain't no game, ain't no play station", Vince the veteran told Peter. "Many of these kids have committed violent acts, even murder to be accepted into the gangs. These are kids struggling to find an identity, with no role models, raised in a society that dehumanised their fathers and feeds them violence for entertainment".

The corrosive effects on their young minds of sustained exposure to unimaginable violence on television, even in jail, was evident to Peter in their manner and the way they talked about doing violence constantly. It was like a drug they were addicted to. At the same time, they were inured to it. To Peter, they were like morons, caught in the vast television wasteland, couch potatoes, moping at the box for hours on end, passively being fed mayhem, murder, rape, gangsters, endless streams of commercials. No brain analysis, no alertness needed, just a barrage of images to be taken in and imitated. Images infinitely closer to reality, *more real than life itself!* Electrical impulses forcing them to create deadly images, scanning their minds, leading their thoughts, enslaving them, *commanding* them, their lives imitating art rather than the other way round.

The effects of television on them were not all that surprising in a country where, to Peter's perception, some people appeared to have so lost sight of reality. Peter had read shocking reports in a magazine about one woman who reportedly paid for a mass at a Catholic church so a TV soap opera couple that broke up could get back together again. In another instance, a five year old, after watching a violent series on television, took his fathers gun, went into the kitchen and shot his mother to death. He could not understand why she didn't get up after seeing the stars that got shot on the *A Team* reappear in the next scene.

Many young gang members Peter met regularly acted out the violence they saw on television -- pretending to shoot defenceless opponents at point blank range, spraying a room full of fellow kids with automatic fire. Air *gun*, not air *guitar!*

As gang members they learned to use a gun, felt the thrill and power of it. Most were unaware of its implications. It was purely a fantasy world. Many came from severely disadvantaged, unsupervised backgrounds. The majority had real problems separating fantasy from reality. They drifted through life in a dream like state, accentuated by the use of hard drugs like crack. They were like denizens of a dark, subterranean nether world where, as one video put it, "only my gun understands me".

Peter was amazed that even in jail, inmates, including violent offenders, were regularly allowed to consume a constant diet of murders, robberies, beatings and muggings on television. Often at the end of a particularly brutal film, he would notice a marked increase in the level of aggressive behaviour. Groups of young inmates would go around the cage barking like dogs, singing soundtracks pulsating with rude raw lyrics, chanting rap songs celebrating guns and death.

It was as if they were being taught desensitisation techniques in jail so they could be sent back into society to commit ever more violent crimes. Peter could see the combined effects of peer and societal pressure on these boys. Many came from families torn apart and the need to be accepted by their peers was strong. The club to be accepted into was the gang and it often forced them to act out the tough guy image -- sometimes to the extent of killing someone. Of course they could not kill as easily in jail. But they could bully and do harmful physical damage.

One fellow who really suffered at their hands was Ngo, the Vietnamese. Peter guessed it was because he was different, the only Oriental in a jail with about one thousand inmates. In addition he was small, less than five foot and quite skinny. When Biter the crime boss discovered Ngo had a real talent for making jailhouse tattoos -- he was the only one who knew how to make and use tattoo guns – he and his gang saw the opportunity to exploit him and like vultures, honed in.

They forced Ngo to draw tattoos on people while they took the payment for themselves -- about three dollars worth of "goodies" made up of mostly potato crisps or candy bars. They were like pimps and Ngo was their whore.

Watching Ngo put together a tattoo gun was like observing a master at work. He would start by making the ink, a process that involved taking the lead out of a pencil and cutting out the metal rim around the eraser. He would use the metal to scrape the side of the lead, turning it into powder and collecting it in a piece of paper. Then he would add a couple drops of shampoo to darken the ink, making it look blue and black when applied to the skin.

To make the gun, he would remove the ink cartridge from the tip of a biro pen, taking care to wash the tip thoroughly. Then he would sharpen a stapler pin to a fine needle - point on the edge of an iron bunk. He would wrap it with thread taken from a prison issue uniform and secure the whole thing -- tip and all -- by forcing it through the ball - point cartridge at the end of the tip. The result was crude but highly effective -- an instant tattoo gun.

The stapler pins were made of stainless steel so they were rust - free and as such were not dangerous.   Peter also learned that the lead from the prison-issue pencils was also not poisonous because it was made from charcoal.   And unless you broke through the inner layer of skin you didn't get blood poisoning.   So care had to be taken to restrict the pricks from the tattoo gun to the outer layer.   It was a delicate job that required skills that only Ngo seemed to possess.   However, Ngo could not keep up with the high demand and crime boss and his cronies began forcing him to reuse the needles, thereby increasing the chances of infection. Sometimes, Ngo would prick the needle a bit too firmly into the skin and blood would trickle out, raising fears of blood contamination.

As Peter discovered, jailhouse tattoos were considered to be extremely cool things to have.   Most inmates marked their skin because they wanted to make a statement or had nothing better to do. Either way, it was extremely popular.

The working class white inmates – so-called white trash -- tended to have more elaborate tattoo designs on their bodies. Some of them looked like they had been spray-painted. They looked like motion graffiti, mobile murals.   One white guy had virtually his entire body tattooed in green, purple and red ink. He looked like a large repellent reptile.

One day Steve, Reid and Peter saw one of Biter's boys – a thug whom they nicknamed Tyson -- roughing Ngo up on instructions from the crime boss. He had apparently said he would no longer do tattoos without getting some remuneration. Peter urged him to report it but Ngo wouldn't snitch.

They decided to start a rumour that Ngo was a black belt but was prevented from taking offensive action because of his Buddhist religion. They made him suddenly leap into the air at strategic moments, making karate like moves and uttering blood curdling howls and chants in Vietnamese. It didn't work. On the contrary, it made things worse for him. Instead of individually, they began to bully him as a group just in case the rumours about his fighting skills turned out to be true.

Peter, Steve and Reid took it upon themselves to make the report to a friendly officer and Ngo was moved to a different floor. Not a moment too soon they thought, but his troubles didn't end there.   There were other members of the same gang on his new floor and one of them attacked him, pouring boiling water all over him.   Fortunately a guard witnessed the incident and his tormentor was sent to "the hole" for twenty days and had a new assault charge added to his already lengthy list of crimes.   Poor Ngo was sent to the hospital cage.

That evening after dinner, Vince and Cecil came over to Peter's corner and he wondered how gang members could be so cruel.

"It's a combination of the effects of drugs, racism and lack of parental care ", Vince said, to which Cecil vigorously nodded his assent.

"Take crack for example. Whoever found it was led by spirits from the pits of hell itself. No narcotic has devastated and robbed man of his spirit and morality like crack. You never found mama leaving her kids for days on end with no diapers or food. She cared too much for her babies. Daddies never used to walk out as much. Crack cocaine destroyed America, robbed it of its spirituality. The spirit to pray, the spirit of respect, of morality. It ravages and destroys everybody that comes across it".

"Add to this the reality of racism for most black Americans", Cecil interjected. "When I was ten they showed us movies about careers in America -- designers, farmers, doctors, engineers and an orchestra performing. I saw this man conducting and I said, 'that's what I want to be, a conductor of a symphony orchestra'. But they said no, you should be in construction or you should become a plumber. That made me to set up a wall and I closed myself off. They thought I was crazy when I started putting tacks on the teacher's chairs and shooting paper clips. So they sent me to a psychiatrist. The doctor gave me drugs to control me and I think that's when my drug dependency began. I've been an addict since I was ten. From that point on it became marijuana, pills, heroin and finally I became a crack head. Society played a part in my addiction".

He cleared his throat and continued.

"You see the elephant? When it's a baby they put one end of a chain around its leg and the other end into the ground. The baby pulls and pulls at it, but can't get it off. When it eventually grows into a huge beast, it does not realise that it can easily pull it out. It merely continues to tug at it and remains chained and in captivity. That's how we are today in the year 2000, as black Americans. Our golden age -- the age of Martin Luther King -- is gone. King was like Tarzan when he makes that call and all the animals listen. When Martin spoke, people of all races listened. Then finally the politicians and the espionage community realised that if they destroyed the man, they would also destroy the movement. So they destroyed him and after they blew his head off, the civil rights movement died. Once they killed him, they killed the dream. Year by year, little by little, the dream died. Now it's as if there was nothing".

He shook his head sadly.

"Equal rights, the little bit they allowed, where is it now? Rosa Parks fought to sit at the front of the bus. Today, black Americans go to sit at the back anyway. The only difference is they appear to be doing it voluntarily. But that is simply conditioning. It's the same reason the elephant won't pull off the chain. As a people we have the same strength to break the chains but we don't".

Vince peeled an orange and began sucking noisily, speaking with his mouth full.

"White America creates the impression that because I'm black, I don't want a house in Beverly Hills and I don't want to feed my kids. That's ridiculous! I call it the dog and bone syndrome. If you have a dog and you beat it everyday, after so long even if you bring the dog its favourite bone it won't come for it because it knows it comes with a beating. It's the same with white America. Everything they give us we pay a terrible price for. So we don't ask for it anymore. We just try and take it through any means possible -- robbery, theft, deception. White America has everything -- finance, schools, everything. We ain't got nothing, so how can they expect us to perform on the same level? That's why these kids are joining gangs, to try and get something through any means possible. Jail don't mean shit to them. Many of these kids had fathers who went to jail and their fathers before them. Prisons and jails in America have historically been filled with black men because of the slave mentality. Lock him up and make him work for us for free again".

He was right when he said there was certainly no shame amongst many inmates for being imprisoned. Recidivism had long since erased the stigma associated with being behind bars. "What you gonna do, send me to jail?" was a popular refrain, often aimed at the guards by a cocky gang member, amid much amusement from the onlookers.

Peter discovered that some inmates were so dirt poor (some of them couldn't afford to pay a $100 bond) they saw incarceration as a cost free way to live for a few weeks or months. To them it was like a summer camp. Some of them invited it by throwing a stone through a car door or walking out of a hamburger joint without paying for the food they'd eaten. They would get arrested and would be given a warm bed, free food and plenty of television. Peter could see how someone without a home and with little prospects, especially in a country with a highly restricted welfare system, would be better off in jail. Compared to those in other parts of the world, American inmates were basically spoiled, though they didn't realise it. What was bad was how the system got them there. But once they were in and could obey the rules, they got comparatively good treatment.

Queensgate was pretty much like a boarding school in a third world country. The main difference was that unlike students, the inmates did no work at all. They were fed, clothed and watered. Their laundry was done for them, corners and halls were cleaned, bathrooms and toilets were spotlessly polished by porters. Unless you were being punished, the only compulsory work was making your bed.

Basic toiletries were supplied free of charge. Additionally, there was the tuck shop where you could buy more expensive soaps and shampoos as well as all the junk food you could afford -- sweets and chocolates, crisps and biscuits, cold and hot beverages and stationery. Each floor had novels, textbooks (excluding law books, apart from the Revised Code mentioned earlier) and newspapers. There were all kinds of games, including chess, draughts, cards and scrabble.

The latest videos were shown at specific times. There was a large viewing area on each floor -- a sort of mini cinema theatre, with two large television sets. TV and phones were usually available from 8am to 11pm, except when inmates were under punishment. Medical facilities were okay, except that the inmate had to pay for it. All floors were fully heated and air-conditioned.

Compare this to prisons and jails in many parts of Europe, particularly the east, where there are still slopping out buckets. And to the developing world, where inmates have to arrange for their own food to be delivered and dozens are kept in cramped cells designed for half their number.

All this of course didn't make the slightest difference to Peter. He found the facilities to be terribly spare and the psychological effects of incarceration, not to mention the ever-present threat of violence from both the guards and inmates, didn't help matters. All he wanted was to regain his freedom and get as far away from there as possible.   But the inmates loved to hear Peter tell them stories about how much better off they were compared to the rest of the world.   At that point they ceased to be black or white, just Americans filled with pride for Uncle Sam.

12

REID WAS HAVING A bad day. He had just finished attacking his third honey bun and was running his banana size finger inside his mouth, picking up bits of food, which he examined almost lovingly before conveying the soggy pulp back into his mouth. After he had sucked on it for a while, Peter watched as he leaned forward and squared himself on his rack, resting his enormous hands on his knees. His fat brow was wrinkled in thoughtful agony. He was facing ten years in prison and his lawyer had just told him the prosecutors would only plea-bargain eight.

Peter could see Reid was crushed. His only option according to his lawyer was to snitch on the guys he got the drugs from. In return, the prosecutors were prepared to reduce his sentence to a maximum of three years. Steve the pseudo hillbilly advised him to squeal only if they were prepared to offer zero jail time, protective custody and change of identity.

"Because let's face it" he said, sipping on his mug of black coffee, "the guys they're asking you to rat on are major drug dealers who will not hesitate to kill and can easily get to you even in jail, or worse to your family". He had a wolfish grin on his face as he watched Reid's eyes darting about nervously. For a fleeting moment, Peter thought he noticed a look of perverse relish on Steve's face as he observed Reid's fear.

Reid was terrified of what might befall his family if he snitched but he was equally scared of being banged up for eight years. Over the next few days, his depression deepened. When he wasn't moaning and feeling thoroughly sorry for himself, he ate massively and continuously, looking more bloated and podgy by the day. In a couple of weeks, he ballooned from 260 to nearly 280 pounds. His belly looked like a balcony over his trousers. It had more than doubled in size, spilling out like a gigantic scrotal sac. His circumference widened considerably and rather than walk, he seemed to roll on his axis, like an ellipsoid. He developed a most unbecoming slouch.

Poor Reid! Peter prayed and talked with him regularly. Peter's problems paled into insignificance compared to Reid's. He was such a good bloke from a very nice family -- a guy who made a mistake that was costing him dearly.

At his request, Peter spoke to Reid's wife and mother on the phone -- a bid to console and give them hope. They tried to sound brave but Peter could tell they were shattered. The unnatural calm in their voices gave away the flustered tension simmering underneath and instantly said they were desperately afraid because they knew that anyway you looked at it Reid was basically screwed.

Reid's mother had been diagnosed with cancer and his arrest had affected her so severely Reid feared he would never see her again as a free man. He also worried about his six-year old son who would be in his teens if Reid got the full sentence.

"This place is a place of the mind", Reid said with a grunt during one of his low moments. "Especially for a man out of his element. Every waking moment, the harsh reality of it is there to crush your spirit. You spend the rest of the day trying to rebuild it only for it to be crushed again. Sometimes I wonder whether I can retain my sanity. Please God, do not change me. Don't turn me into one of these animals. Let me keep my faith, my identity, my innocence, my good nature. All that is me. What's the use of coming out still breathing but it ain't you no more? It's a very scary thought. I think I'd prefer to lose my life. It's incredible the ups and downs. It rips at your whole being. It's so damn hard to look at the bright side of things when all that's around you is sadness. Where does one find strength day to day to keep going? I would rather work ten hours a day in a coal mine. Here you have to wake up everyday and try to figure out how to make yourself happy. What do I do today? Pick my toe nails, comb my hair?"

Tears clouded his eyes, coursing down his lugubrious face. Peter tried to smile reassuringly at him. But Reid was utterly inconsolable. He had tried to take a short cut in life and it had turned out to be the longest way round.

"Every time I go to court -- good spirited, gung-ho -- I've come back beaten down. Other people seem to have the good and the bad, the wins and losses, but in my case it's been bad news every time. I see the CO's flashlight in my face telling me 'you've got court today'. I'm like 'oh no, not court.' What do they want today? My arm, my foot or part of my ear lobe? I come back from court, picking up what's left of my pride, dragging it behind me. I had hoped that today the prosecutors would understand I'm just a man. A man with a family, a man with a life too. I try to tell them but they won't listen. How do you appeal to a system that doesn't care about those things? The judgements are too black and white. You did this and that's it -- you get that! I don't care whether you've got ten children. We'll get that money and time out of your carcass. And so a good man gets sent in. And he comes out bitter and corrupt".

The hapless Californian shook his great leonine head sadly and stuffed another jolly rancher into his mouth. Peter worried about the state of his fat heart.

"This thing they call rehabilitation", he said with dismay. "It's about as much rehab as a lobotomy. Except a lobotomy will probably be better human rights. They should at least take the pain away. Keep me in cryogenics. All they've got to do is keep the liquid nitrogen going. It's cheaper too but they won't do it because it's not painful enough".

The tears flowing fast and thick now!

"Dear Lord, please don't fight me. I don't want you to carry me on your back, but please give me a break. My suffering is already a big test. If it was just me it would perhaps be okay. But my family! Please, ease their pain. I haven't actually tallied in my mind how long eight years is. Eighty percent chance my mom won't be here. What will my child feel for me when I come out? How he adores his dad now. It ain't gonna be like that then. Two years or even three could have been enough for a first time offender. But these bastards aren't happy until they ruin a person's life. Eight years! I feel anger and bitterness for the system and this whole damn country. There's a whole range of emotions. On one side of the coin there's anger. On the other, utter grief. Grief that runs deep to the bone, ripping at my very soul! No matter what I do, I can't get rid of this hurt. It follows me around like a ball and chain tied to my leg"

Reid was so depressed Peter feared he would do something crazy. Steve and Peter began keeping watch over him. But they need not have worried. Reid's faith, though severely tested, remained firm. He was very Catholic and he believed strongly in the Blessed Virgin Mary and that all the saints of heaven were looking out for him, especially Saints Joseph and Anthony.

13

REID'S WOES DID NOT make Peter's any easier. He existed in a vale of misery as he watched people come and go.

In the time Peter was there, hundreds travelled through the Queensgate system. People constantly moving in and out! Those found guilty were transferred to prisons and up state penitentiaries to do their penance. Every evening a new replacement unit of offenders arrived. An assemblage of misfits trooped in formation and commanded by a Queensgate garrison guard. *Legion of Vice!* Some Peter saw more than once, mostly those arrested for violating their probation. But always, the traffic, the *slavery*, continued! People arrested on the slightest pretext. A city earning its keep from arrests!

It was no longer the People with a large *P* versus particular individuals. It was particular individuals, specifically unscrupulous Prosecutors versus the people, who the *Persecutors* had tin-snipped to a very slight, greatly reduced *p*. The people had clearly lost to the dictatorship of a clique of politicians determined to maintain their hold on power. The very pinnacles of propriety and integrity, driven by greed, ambition and cruelty, just like the criminals they were supposed to be protecting the people from.

Take the case of the 38-year old Latino Peter met at Queensgate called Carlos. At twenty-eight, he was found guilty of selling drugs and was sent to Mansfield penitentiary in Ohio, an old style prison where in those days if you were taken to the hole you were likely to receive electric shocks. When he went in, he had a baby who was seven months old. After he served ten years and got out, he was promptly re-arrested and brought in front of a judge in Cincinnati who told him he owed thousands of dollars in child support arrears and that his ex-wife had been on welfare. He tried to explain to the judge that he had been incarcerated.

"You put me in jail for 10 years and that's why my former wife went on welfare". The judge replied: "That's not my problem. You owe child support".

And they tossed him right back into jail. How can such a system be fair, Peter wondered?

"The people now have no choice but to take their chances with the dictatorship and hope they can get away on a plea or a fine", Robert told Peter with a frown, after hearing Carlos's story. "The original concept of "We the People" is lost on this city and county".

His words made it all sound bleaker than ever to Peter. And if like him, "We the People" happened to be a non-American, an *alien,* then you were well and truly in bad nick. You were subjected to a very public vilification - this hell he was now living in -- and the information you supplied in defence of yourself suppressed by them. The worst crime and the greatest dishonesty coming from the very pillars of justice, integrity and impartiality that "We the People" had entrusted with the defence of their cause and the protection of the concept of innocent until proven guilty. Justice was certainly not a blind folded woman in Peter's case, but an ambition politician with wide-open, greedy eyes set on re-election. The *man* and his cohorts should be the ones on trial for betraying the trust of "We the People".

"It is no longer ' "We the People" '. More like ' "We the Government" or "We the Political Clique" ', Robert said, his eyes flashing angrily. They were headed into the sunshine for one hour of outside recreation allowed every three days.

"Not just in Cincinnati but in many cities across America. That's why ' "We the People" ' are beginning to rebel. That's why militias are springing up around the country. ' "We the People" ' want our country back. ' "We the People" ' want our rights back. We want to return to good old-fashioned values. Not the invented values of politicians they feed us on their campaign trail, but the true values and principles on which this country was founded. Government *of* the People *for* the People and *by* the People!"

Peter learned that there were groups of people prepared to fight against the government, who felt the authorities had pushed them to the limit and the people no longer had any rights to speak of. The rising number of incidents of random violence carried out by regular Americans showed clearly how frustrated many people had become in the "land of the free".

"The ordinary people no longer seem able to use the legal system to fight against injustice", Robert continued. "The system is being used against them. Many people, including the guards here, complain that taxes and fines have become outrageously high. Yet the United States fought for independence from Britain because of high taxes and fines. This country has turned into a police state and the police and government prosecutors can do whatever they want. The government is even allowing the police to videotape people they arrest -- people who should be innocent until proven guilty -- and to sell these videos for entertainment on television, possibly violating the constitutional rights of citizens".

They sat down on the grass verge next to the basket ball court. Vince who had been trailing behind joined them. The sadness in his eyes made Peter uncomfortable. His voice quavered, sounding cracked as if he was about to break into tears. A man battling extreme stress!

"I was in court today and all of a sudden I started thinking.

How could these judges and prosecutors treat us like this, especially poor black people who have no money to defend themselves? Knowing they are destroying our hopes, causing catastrophe in our lives. Just another days work. Those people don't feel for their fellow human beings. When I walked out of the lift, I saw nothing but black people -- the families of inmates. What really hurt was that they didn't feel out of place. It seemed normal, like ' "we accept our plight" ' with no resistance, like a slave accepting the wishes of the master. Walking through there in handcuffs, I fitted right in, just one of the boys. No one batted an eyelid. I thought, how could man not love his fellow man? How could they despise us so much, just because of our colour and our poverty, that they'd go to any lengths to destroy whatever prospects we have?"

Robert nodded. "I think it is modern day slavery and poor blacks as well as non blacks are back on the plantation", he said, shaking his head sadly. "The Ham County criminal justice system is a business that also treats many poor whites most unfairly. There are as many penitentiaries here in Ham and the rest of Ohio as there are in Texas, a state that's ten times its size. Every time someone is sent to the penitentiary, black or white, the state pays the county hard dollars. Every time a child support case is successfully prosecuted, the prosecutor is paid a percentage of the money recovered. That is why they connive with the women to exaggerate the man's earnings and inflate the figures. Then they scare the shit out of you by making you feel you could never win. Of course the reason you are not paying in the first place is often because you can't afford the huge amount they have fabricated and claim that you owe. You can't afford a private lawyer so you have a public prosecutor, supposedly your defender, who is on their payroll, and he urges you to plea bargain your rights away or risk being put away and still have to pay when you get out".

Vince agreed, squinting his eyes against the sunlight.

"If more people went to trial rather than took a plea, forcing the state to pay all that money for a trial, then they wouldn't arrest so many people and the numbers of people in prison, especially blacks, would start to fall".

Peter closed his eyes. *Oh America, choking with transgression! I could never understand you. Nor would I ever understand how fate had seen it fit to let you dominate my world these past few months, my lifeblood spilling, your victim unwilling!*

Peter opened his eyes and resolved that something positive would come out of this. A phoenix would rise out of the ashes of his tragedy. King Shaka, in a rustic land, would fight against the dominion Yokels who had fastened a wooden crosspiece over his neck. But would he win?

14

EARLY MORNING. A TWILIGHT zone, dream-like state when Peter is undisturbed. His own space, virginal! Then the lights come on, the tannoy crackles and the perspective changes. *Please leave me in peace!*

"Razor call! Razor call! You got fah minutes to pick up your razors, shave and bring em back. Fah minutes! It's razor call assholes! C'mon, let's, move it you fuck heads!"

Cheap *used* bic shavers! Afterwards, Peter feels like his face could sand down a coffee table. If he'd attempted to shave any closer, he'd have no skin left. He'd have torn it right off.

The guard with the wicked gleam was sounding particularly disagreeable this morning. He had been dozing on his desk having had a riotous drunken bout and been dragged into work the same evening with his head throbbing. He snapped and snarled viciously, like an angry Doberman Pinscher and didn't seem to realise or care that everyone was shooting him down with eyes of hate. A rumble of suppressed anger rolled around the cage like thunder.

For Peter, another day at Queensgate, his place of confinement, stretched out forlornly. The day was turning into days, days into weeks, weeks dragging by, refusing to be hurried along. It was like being in a slow motion film in which Peter was aware that he was moving at a greatly reduced pace but his mind still operated at normal speed.

Every night Peter watched the moon playing hide and seek with the clouds. During the day, he watched the seasons pass. He watched the moon and the seasons pass. It felt like seasons because through the barred windows, he observed the rain and then the sun changing places every week. For several days, there would be brilliant dazzling sunshine without a cloud in the sky. Then suddenly a shadow would fall across the world, blocking out the sun behind storm clouds. Then lightning flashed, thunder rumbled and the rains fell, sometimes heavily, other times in light drizzle, reminding him of England.

Peter loved watching the rain. It calmed his nerves. As some writer put it, it showered a beautiful peace on things. The whole world as far as Peter's eye could see from behind the meshed windows became wet. Nothing escaped!

The venom spewed in Peter's direction by the media had slowed. For the moment there was nothing to report until the next court appearance. The inmates however remained a menace, exploiting the environment, threatening to rip out the throats of those who stood in the way. They were the biggest problem Peter faced, along with boredom, loneliness and a profound sense of helplessness. He was at their mercy and that of the garrison guards, the prosecutors, his lawyer and the judge.

Everything crawled. Even his nerves jangled more slowly, less frequently, although they stayed rattled. He became more contemplative, but the further he reflected on things the more depressed he became. His dream, his goal of becoming a permanent news anchor on the world's most watched network which had literally been within his grasp, stolen away from him by a cruel fortune, perhaps never again to be attained. The fabric of his life, torn to shreds! His melancholy worsened, brooding over him like a hen protecting her chicks with a covering of its wings.

The waiting for something to happen, the constant hope that an unexpected, improbable event would provide a sudden solution to his difficulty -- his *deus ex machina* -- was the most difficult and demanding aspect of it all for Peter. It was not his favourite thing. He had always been the impatient sort, driven by a perfectionist streak in his chosen profession. The challenge of keeping himself occupied and motivated tried him beyond words. He was morose and gloomy. His melancholy loomed enormously like a mountain.

Peter slept! Thick night, bringing twisted tortured dreams! He awoke to the crackle of the tannoy, ordering everyone to pack up "immediately". Without warning or notice. They suddenly had to move down to the 4th floor because someone had decided the 7th floor needed to be renovated.

Through the kind, unsolicited action of one sympathetic guard, Reid became Peter's new corner mate. They both welcomed it, especially as they occupied the "penthouse" -- the area closest to the windows -- and began enjoying a modestly attractive view of the Ohio riverbank and the headlands of Kentucky.

Reid's crisis had deepened. The police were threatening to arrest his wife as an accomplice to his crime and take his child into foster care. They had apparently gone to his house for a "routine" search and she had refused to let them in. They threatened to break down the door and take her away in front of their six-year old son but she wouldn't budge. Then they went away and waited for her at their son's school and slapped handcuffs on her as she arrived to pick him up. So she eventually let them in.

Reid could barely control the furious intensity of his rage.

"In front of everyone they cuffed her. They had no right to do that because she had nothing to do with my indictment. What was she going to do -- a woman, run away from four male cops? If I could, I would have sent a lightning bolt down to fry them on the spot. It's like the KGB saying if you don't build this bomb, we'll send your family to Siberia. The particular detective who made all the threats was the same one who arrested me. His heart is so cold you could chill a six pack of beer next to it".

Reid roll hopped nervously from one foot to the other.

"This *is* the Great Satan -- not the people, but the government and police. They have to be. They have no humanity, no souls. They remind me of the terminator. Everyone's just doing their jobs without feelings, ruining people's lives."

The day that began uneventfully had been stained with this unexpected downer. Reid's mood plunged. Peter wished he could find a way to ease his friend's heartache, but of course there wasn't. All he could do was listen as Reid continued sadly.

"Now I see the police as the enemy never to be trusted again. They expect kids to look up to them yet they do this in front of a six-year old. How could he ever look up to them again? He's been scarred by it and my wife tells me that every time he sees a police car he hides under the seat. I don't like them anymore. I don't trust them. I find myself wondering if someone had a problem whether I'd direct them to ask cops for help because I don't know what I'd be getting them into. Once the police are involved it could become a nightmare. I sit here with my life in limbo. My family are living with their hearts skipping every other beat because they don't know whether or when they'll see me again. I hope those cops burn in hell".

15

DESPITE THE LEADEN GLOOM that pervaded Peter's time at Queensgate, there were odd moments of great mirth.

Prurient stories were a popular form of entertainment. Dirty storytellers and lavatory humorists were held in high esteem. *Man, I spread that bitch like the wings of a fucking eagle!* Sex -- or the absolute absence of it -- in an open jail such as Queensgate was a rare and celebrated thing and there were moments of sexual hilarity. Peter was amazed at how the sighting of anything female easily caused the sea of delinquency to surge, starting something of a flood in which you risked being drowned. As the news got around, herds of inmates would stampede across the dormitory, leaping over racks, bounding across lockers, fighting to secure a choice position by the window. Cat calls, whistles and every conceivable obscenity would be hurled at the women on the streets, some of whom clearly enjoyed the attention.

On one occasion, an inmate who was nicked for pimping convinced his honey skinned Narragansett "squaw" and her dusky hirsute Latin friend – his "butch bitches" as he called them -- to turn up outside the meshed windows and put on a show for the boys. They appeared at the appointed time -- about 100 yards away -- and tore off their bras in one pre-rehearsed motion. They both had ample breasts and as they shook and wiggled their generous jugs amorously the whole building erupted in cheers and shouts of "tit-fuck...tit-fuck...tit-fuck", everyone swaying their hips or tossing their joss - sticks to the rhythm.

Another time, a white girl of about nineteen who had recently started whoring with the same pimp took off all her clothes and the inmates went wild. Some of the younger ones grabbed the barred windows, pulled down their trousers and thrust their eye-poker hard-ons forward with sexual suggestiveness. While she was flashing her luscious form and enjoying all the attention, the Corrections Officers went round the back threw a sheet over her and detained her until the police arrived. But the girl had made everyone's day and her glorious curves were the topic of discussions, many wet dreams and much jerking off for weeks on end.

Once in the wee hours of the morning when nothing, not even the guard stirred, Peter went to the bathroom to ease himself and stumbled upon two blokes naked from the waist down, caressing each other, both very erect. He stared at them and they quickly moved apart, fleeing back to their racks. For the rest of Peter's time at Queensgate they avoided him. That was the closest he ever came to observing any homosexual activity, although a number of inmates were clearly inclined in that direction the way they shimmied around the place. He never saw any heterosexual action either, in spite of rumours and gossip about inmates bribing the guards to bring whores or their girlfriends into Queensgate.

But *auto* sexuality – masturbation -- was fairly common especially after lights out. It was not unusual to detect squirming movements under the sheets accompanied sometimes by the occasional moan and heavy breathing. Look closely and you'd see turgescent swellings sticking up from under blankets lightly illuminated by corridor lights. The "wankers" and there were several on any night, would catch their semen in toilet paper and toss the used tissue onto the floor, well away from their racks. In the morning when the porters swept and polished, they often found tufts of toilet tissue stuck to the floor. Once an angry bellow erupted from an outraged cleaner that cut across the cage.

"Whose been choking their motherfucking chicken?" followed by ripples of laughter.

"Motherfucker" was without doubt the most popular expletive in use at Queensgate. Virtually every half sentence contained the word. Somehow it had managed to insinuate itself into all forms of usage. Peter wondered how such a term *mother - fucker* came into existence. No one seemed to know where it came from, though some of the older inmates recalled hearing it used first in the late 1950s, then later in blaxploitation movies like *Shaft* in the early 1970s.

Toileting was always one of the more difficult aspects of being in a county jail. One part most people don't like to show anyone else is *that*. Which is why people lock the door when they go to the loo (the john in the US). At Queensgate, there was no bathroom door to lock. Everything was open and there was absolutely no privacy. The toilets were built opposite the row of urinals and you were in full view of anyone urinating or walking past.

Peter felt humiliated and diminished by it. He tried to get up early to do it when it was least embarrassing. He used to time himself to go just after breakfast -- around 6.00am -- because most people usually went back to sleep after eating. Pretty soon, he found out that many people were on the same clock and had similar ideas.

Peter made some truly serendipitous discoveries at Queensgate, one of them being a recipe for possibly the most effective cold remedy he had ever come across. Squeeze the yellow outer rind of an orange (not the edible citrus fruit inside) into a cup. Add boiling water and maybe a little bit of sugar or honey. Let it sit for about 3 minutes and drink it. Do this twice on the first day you start to feel the cold and it should all be over by the next day.

He also discovered a very doughy concoction created by the

inmates called "break" -- the jailhouse equivalent of a pizza or thick savoury flan. It looked nasty but had a nice flavour, a sort of coarse, clodhopper distinction that went rather well with that unsettled environment. It consisted of an improbably hectic mix of cooked food and commissary provisions -- barbecue crisps, bologna bummed from the porters, bread and hot dogs and burgers heisted from the chow hall, pickle juice, soup, "cat food", cookies and whatever else they could lay their hands on. They would mix it all up, their dirty fingers sinking in, kneading it into dough then pulling it apart, putting it together and tossing it like a pizza. Slowly, a most extraordinary metamorphosis would occur -- something like a close relative of a dumpling or a quiche or unleavened bread would emerge. It was a bit like eating chocolate chip dough with a more rustic very filling taste, sticking to the ribs.

However, for the amount of hassle that was expended making it, especially trying to get past the guards with hot dogs and burgers in your socks, Peter thought it was a bloody waste. Besides, it somehow seemed to legitimise the environment. *Grab a pew! Won't you stay for supper? We are home!*

The recidivists and long stay inmates who had become used to life behind bars were usually most adept at creating such things. They were like walking ids, seeking what little gratification they could squeeze out of their vagrant surroundings. They would make toast by lighting toilet paper under a piece of bread. Some even had barbecues, smuggling raw meat in from the kitchen and using one of the iron bunks as a cooking pan. They would heat it up with a stolen lighter and lots of paper and presto! Before your very eyes, rare steak!

Rumour had it that smuggling of another kind also took place regularly.

"For fifty dollars, a guard can bring in cigarettes and a lighter", Steve said, hopped to the eyes as usual on black coffee. "You could get marijuana for one hundred dollars. All you gotta do is get friends or relatives on the outside to deliver the money to the officer".

He leaned closer and whispered:

"If you've got five hundred dollars, you could get some pussy. Your girl or a whore could come in here. For one thousand dollars, you could get an overnight guest. With enough money, one of the guards would let you out -- even set you free. That's how corrupt the system is".

Every kind of medicament contraband was available for a price. Peter saw inmates smoking cigarettes, marijuana and crack. There seemed to be more drugs inside the correctional system per square mile than outside and some of the guards were said to be the agent provocateurs, the facilitators who made it happen.

16

P<small>ETER IS LYING ON</small> his back reading Slyvia Plath's villanelle.

"I shut my eyes and all the world drops dead. I lift my lids and all is born again (I think I made you up inside my head)".

Images of eyes closing in death and opening into birth floated in and out of his consciousness. Outside the meshed windows, summer beckoned. Inside, tribes of raptorial inmates rushed past Peter's sleeping quarters. The indignity of man in defeat! The spirit, fractured and torn by adversity, no longer functioning properly having crossed the thin line of resiliency and now out of working order. How was it supposed to bounce back from misfortune? *I am hurt, stung, assailed, but I am not slain. I will bleed awhile, allow great gushes of blood to issue forth from me, then I'll rise, but will I be able to fight again?*

Dear Juliet

I have been walking dead for nearly a month now, like the corpse of a voodoo zombie, stalled at lichgate, awaiting the clergyman's arrival. The outside, the world beyond these bars and wires, this calaboose dungeon, exists only in collect calls and through your letters.

The rest is pure imagination. I have come to know this unreality like the back of my hand. I regularly disappear into it. At each sudden unsteady flare, I make copious notes in my paper notebook, but also in the notebook of my mind that I bury deep, to be exhumed at a later time. I am forced to create vast reaches between this hellish community and me. It is the only way I can remain characteristic of a person, as opposed to an animal.

Tonight I hold you close.

17

In spite of all its flaws and infirmities, Peter found that if you looked hard enough, there was also a tempering element and enough energy and dash to keep one from going under in that place. The few "Bible thumpers" who truly believed provided him with a courageous inspiration. As he stumbled along, they helped him discover a vitally transforming essence and a great faith was stirred in him.

It was probably the fact that his future was scudding along in the hands of others -- his cadaverous lawyer, the establishment judge, the astoundingly ambitious prosecutor, the *woman* -- all of them twisting his life about for publicity and for money. Holding his life in their hands, singing his requiem, orchestrating his *auto-da-fe*.

His family he trusted, especially his fiancée Juliet and his sister Priscilla, the two women who bore his leaden distress -- *my hurt that hurtled rapidly with a clattering sound* -- both solid as a rock against his monstrous affliction. *The death thy death hath dealt to me is greater than the death thy death has dealt to thee.*

Juliet's flood of letters -- sometimes up to four a week -- and Peter's almost daily collect calls to Priscilla, sustained his spirit. Kept him keeping on. And there was his brother Zik a few miles away in Columbus, and his other brother Chu, soon to arrive Cincinnati from his university in Leicestershire, England, to lend support. But even they could not totally appreciate what he was going through. There was only one to whom he could completely give his sorrows: the Great Spirit in the Sky.

Peter began to read constantly about a Jewish Carpenter named Joshua Ben Yosef who lived 2000 years ago. No matter how horrific Peter's hurt, it could not compare to Joshua's. The Romans insulted him and beat him. They accused him of crimes he did not commit and bore false witness against him. Then they tortured him some more, crowned his head with thorns and hammered him to a cross to die a slow and awful death. Peter could only imagine the man's suffering in those days after his capture, when there were no human rights commissions or civil rights groups. He must have literally descended into hell.

Consider Joshua, immersed in passion and pain. How rough the Roman soldiers must have been two thousand years ago when today we still complain about police brutality. Dragged off, beaten, abused and deserted by his companions. Jailed in unspeakably harsh conditions. Locked down in a dungeon. Talk about the hole! Paraded, vilified and scourged some more, finally condemned to death. Forced to carry his cross and to lie on it as large nails were hammered into his hands, his ankles broken so they could bend his feet for the nails. Then hoisted up for hours, arms aching from the weight, side pierced with a lance, thirst deepening with vinegar thrust in his mouth, under a relentless sun.

Yet he forgave his tormentors. Who was he Peter to complain? Who was he to ask "why me", to demand progress without pain, to call for "Easter without Good Friday?"

Most of his adult life Peter had been a lolloping agnostic, choosing to straddle the fence between non-belief and belief. Sometimes he veered dangerously to the left. But for the first time, he felt himself inclining to the "right path of rectitude", as his father would say.

18

In the last week of May, Dan, a Nigerian lawyer based in Hamilton County arranged for Peter to meet Len Dobson, a high powered trial lawyer.

Dobson was a real "celebrity attorney", one of a new breed of made-for-television legal eagles like Johnny Cochran. He acquired the nickname "Pit Bull" because he was noted for his ferocity when on a case, snapping at the heels of the prosecution until he won. His paid advertisements took it a step further, describing him as the American Pit Bull Terrier who would fight for his clients like a junkyard dog or something along those lines. Dan thought he was the perfect firebrand who could take on the establishment and win.

Dobson rarely lost a case and had gained publicity by representing many high profile clients. He was popular with the press and was often in the news, a natural representative of those the seemingly unassailable power structure wanted to put away. He was disliked by establishment figures -- the Judges and Prosecutors. A revolutionary lawyer and a maverick, Dobson was an American version of Britain's Lord Gifford (a criminal lawyer and pioneer in human rights and legal reform, with particular experience in representing victims of racism and discrimination, as well as political prisoners) and the establishment not only hated his guts, they feared him mainly because he didn't fear them.

To make matters worse for the Cincinnati establishment, he was the inheritor of the chambers and mantle of Isaiah James Fitzpatrick, a respected black lawyer who became a famous Hamilton County judge and suddenly gave it all up to become a preacher.

Ordinary people -- black and white -- greatly admired Dobson for his guts and he was something of a folk hero, especially with the formidable aura of Judge Pastor Fitzpatrick hanging over him.

"I read about your case in the newspapers and Dan told me about you", Len Dobson said, beaming as he sat down with Peter in the meeting room at Queensgate. "Why don't you tell me the whole story?"

Peter found he instantly liked Dobson. He was confident without being over bearing and he possessed an enthusiasm and zest for life that inspired confidence and a feeling of camaraderie. He listened patiently as Peter told his story. Peter felt a growing sense of hope.

"You've got to understand it's no longer just a child support case", he said, looking at Peter with evident sincerity. "This is politics. It's on TV and they've got elections coming up".

He rose to his feet.

"They want you badly brother and they are going to do everything to send you to the pen. They think they can put you away for at least two years. Or that they'll be able to extract a large amount of money from you. That's why they made a big show of your arrest and extradition and this bond nonsense. It's a tough case but we've got a good chance because you've got truth on your side. But I'm gonna tell you straight up. It's gonna cost you a few thousand dollars".

Peter's sense of hope dissipated considerably when Len mentioned money. Several grand in legal fees in addition to that already spent on the cadaver. Oodles of boodle for the Pit Bull and no guarantees! *And so I sit here wringing my hands, uttering mea culpas while you count your dosh.*

"There's only one way to do it", Dobson continued, cocking his head, his eyes lighting up. "Fight! To clear your name! To stop what is happening to you happening to others! We're gonna go to trial by a jury that's not politically motivated and we're gonna win".

There's that confidence again. Hope rising!

"We will defeat them and you will leave here in triumph. If we have to we'll put up a fierce constitutional challenge. In this country, cases have changed the law and the courts can overturn laws made by the legislature".

Peter took a deep breath and sat back to look at the man into whose hands he was commending his fate. He was a pleasant looking chap in his late thirties, about five foot ten with a beige brown face, curly hair and large white teeth. Peter made up his mind right there to hire him.

"Can you get me out on bond?" Peter asked. "I'm going absolutely potty in here".

"We can certainly try", he said, "But a bond reduction is up to the judge who happens to be a politician" he continued. "So don't hold your breath. As I said, your best shot is with a jury at a trial. It may take a bit of time before you get out, but you are gonna get out a free man. I cant guarantee it but I can feel it and I've been in this business long enough to trust my instincts. So you're just gonna have to trust me".

And with that he shook Peter's hand and was gone. It wasn't a particularly up beat note on which to end their discussions, but Peter felt Dobson had been honest and straight and most of all, he felt he could trust him.

Soon after Dobson left, Peter got a surprise visit.

"Someone to see you, Sir Peter", said the tiny elfish guard with a round face that everybody called Shorty.

"Who could it be?" Peter wondered aloud, knowing it couldn't possibly be his new lawyer because he had just left.

"An old friend it seems", said Shorty.

Peter ran down the four flights of stairs to the visiting pen in the basement. He looked through the glass partition at the red head with a broad smile.

"Tina", he said in amazement. She blew him a kiss.

"I read about you in the newspapers. I've been trying to reach you for the last two days. I went to the Justice Centre but they said you were here and by the time I arrived yesterday it was too late. I hope you don't mind my coming to see you".

Peter was touched. "No, not at all", he replied quickly.

Tina was an American red head of Italian descent. They had met nearly twenty years ago as students at Xavier University. Peter last saw her three years before in Rome, where she had been on assignment as a reporter for National Public Radio, the respected American network. He would not have guessed she was anywhere near Cincinnati if she had simply left without seeing him. He was touched and turned away so she could not see the tears welling up in his eyes.

For the rest of her stay in Cincinnati -- about a week, Tina came to see him every other day, providing him with a steady supply of reading and writing material. When she left for Rome, she offered her flat in Cincinnati free of charge for Peter and members of his family to stay, in case they came to visit. When his younger brother, Chu, arrived from England two weeks later, he spent over a month in her neat little apartment and Peter also stayed there for a couple of days before returning to England. Peter resolved to someday return Tina's kindness.

19

June 9th!

The day of Peter's second bond hearing arrived and a dark brooding cloud hung over him as he prepared for court. In spite of all the prayers and faith and hope from Juliet and Priscilla, neither Dobson nor anyone else could predict which way the cat would jump. Each meeting with Dobson leading up to the hearing offered only limited amounts of hope and bags of depression. What was particularly disheartening was Dobson's insistence on playing the devil's advocate and laying all the cards on the table.

As the days dragged on and the hearing approached, Peter became short tempered, irritable and withdrawn, much to the disappointment of people like Reid, who looked to him as a "picker upper", as he put it.

Even the photo of herself Juliet had sent him, which would normally cheer him up did nothing to pull him out of his despondency. Peter could tell his sister Priscilla, with whom he was in constant telephone communication, was also uncomfortable with the apparent lack of certainty, though she tried hard to impress upon him that even if they lost, it would only be a temporary set back, as Dobson himself had pointed out. She hadn't and would not lose faith. What a trooper!

After weeks of waiting, Peter was finally sitting in the holding pen, preparing to board the mobile cage along with about twenty-five other inmates for the drive to the Justice Centre. A dagger in the form of the mush he had for breakfast attacked his stomach, forcing it to rumble threateningly. He was allowed to go to the toilet. By the time he returned fifteen minutes later the inmates were in single file, chained to each other hand to hand, slowly boarding the mobile cage.

The beer-bloated blimp called Larry was barking commands indignantly. His enormous, ponderous gut spilled out over the top half of his trousers, as if it was about to burst from viviparous pressure. Most of his head was bare of hair. What little there was – dark threadlike erectile strands – grew on the back of his neck, rising when he spoke, like the feathered hackles on the saddle of a domestic rooster. His restless eyes searched the faces of the inmates rapaciously -- a vulture hunting for carrion to tear into. They rested on Peter and the Carthartidae closed in.

"What's that in your pocket?" His voice sounded loud, brittle and hostile.

Before Peter could answer, Larry reached into his breast pocket, removed the statement he had carefully prepared to read to the court in mitigation of his high bond and threw it into the bin. A profane disregard! An unwarranted violation! Gratuitous disrespect! Peter was on the verge of attacking him but the thought of wrestling with about ten guards armed with guns and billy clubs forced him to restrain his resentment.

"I told everyone to remove papers from their pockets, including court papers", Larry continued, glaring at Peter.

"I was in the toilet and I didn't hear. Your colleague here gave me permission to go". Peter looked imploringly at the other guard who ignored him.

"You can report me to the judge", Larry replied savagely and cuffed him. Peter tried to remain calm but inside he choked with hate and anger. He was greatly discouraged by this development and his spirit plunged. Everywhere he looked that morning a veil of darkness enveloped even the brightest spark of hope. The scales seemed to dip rather dangerously against him and he felt that even God was on the verge of deserting him. All he could do was wait and hope.

20

LATE MORNING!

Peter, led by a guard, entered the courtroom. Once again the cameras were poking their snouts everywhere, blasting him with flashlights and floodlights -- a wall of brilliant illumination practically demolishing him with its vigour and dazzle, forcing him to wince. The avenging press and that distasteful prosecutor, once again embedding their talons with destructive intent in his life, people at whose feet his decimated world now lay and who had declared war on him.

Prosecutio assinus est... the prosecutor is an ass...Nevertheless... *nos morituri te salutamus...* we who are about to die, salute you! He couldn't get beyond that, couldn't seem to remember how to spell much less convey Latin subjects and predicates or whatever any more. He was stuck. There was a time, in fact up until a few weeks ago, when he could easily whip up any number of Latin sentences. But all of a sudden, after his brain had gained admission into this trauma centre, after his world had shrunk and had been firmly secured in a straitjacket by them, it had vanished.

And now in the full prime of his dotage, he was pitifully, shamefully trying to do his Latin declension and finding himself caught. Trapped in this double entendre! Flailing about in a dead language syntactic nightmare, battling with the variation of the form of a noun, pronoun or adjective. He couldn't even remember how to conjugate simple words like mensa, divinus or was it *divius* Persecutor! Persecuteur! Persequi...sequi...secut...whatever.

Peter glared at the prosecutor -- *You did this to me!* – then at the guards and then at his defence team, taking turns. His eyes were suddenly opened to a whole new seething underworld of lawyers, prosecutors and judges, police and corrections officers. Errant thoughts of voluptuous violence darted in and out of his mind. Bilious anger rushed through his system as he watched them. They were taking it all so lightly, speaking so casually and amiably to each other -- these lawyers and prosecutors and policemen -- while he stood to one side, shackled, fettered, restrained, his fate hanging in the balance, his future all but destroyed by this cataclysmic upheaval. He found it even more galling that Dobson, into whose hands he had commended his life, actually found something to chuckle about with *them*.

Peter turned to the stenographer or court reporter as the Americans called them, a sad looking woman in her fifties with mournful puppy dog eyes and wattled cheeks, who was staring at him with what appeared to be a mixture of pity and revulsion. Peter glared back at her with all the menace he could muster. She shrank back into her chair and quickly looked away. For the rest of the time she stole furtive sideways glances at him.

The judge entered the courtroom and smiled reassuringly at Peter. *A great weight lifted from his shoulders.* Then shortly after statements from Dobson and the prosecutors, Judge Burrows dropped the bomb. He would not reduce the bond because, he said, the prosecution had demonstrated clearly that Peter remained a flight risk. *The weight toppled from its height, crashing back down onto his shoulders.*

The court reporter, casting darting glances at him again. Swift, passing quickly over him. What was she thinking? Not that it mattered anyhow, but he found himself to be curious. He sucked his lower lip. It tasted oddly sweet! How strange! And all the while he stood there, a living, walking nightmare in cuffs, dressed in correctional facility standard issue clothing, humiliated, watching the nails -- huge six inch nails -- being hammered into his coffin. Nothing to hold onto, nothing of his life was left. Nothing of his original self meant anything. He was a prisoner…*their* prisoner and that was all he was. He belonged to the state. The world he used to know before no longer existed.

Peter left the courtroom as he entered it -- in cuffs. Behind him, the guard set the pace, maintaining a tight grip on his arm. As they reached the door, he tried to turn to glimpse his brother Zik who had driven down from Columbus to attend the hearing, but the guard growled at him. They went through the door beyond which no free person could pass and the outside world disappeared.

Peter was back in the subterranean domain. *Desaparecido,* existing in the concealed realm of the disinherited! Before him, a world of chains and cages, recidivists and Corrections Officers, cut off from the sunlight, into a dimmer, gloomier artificial brightness. Except for the small barred windows sitting high above on the outer walls of the court house, through which he could hear the low murmur of distant traffic and see rays of light, the world he used to know was lost, excluded, banished, far removed. The end of that world! And now, this one had intruded.

Peter's head was spinning. How could this be happening to him? Riding high in April, shot down suddenly in May, walking wounded in June and now they were preparing to bury him alive in July, casually hammering six-inch nails into his coffin. How had he ended up in this intolerable condition, this cataclysm? How could he suddenly be in Cincinnati, a long, long way from his home in England? Worse, how could he be in handcuffs in a courtroom under the full glare of cameras?

Simple! Malice aforethought! Contrived by the prosecutor

using the *woman*. You did this to *me*! He who had just been presenting the news on the world's most watched network. Was this a movie or a trick? But the courtroom didn't resemble a set. He had seen several and this certainly wasn't one. The policemen with their guns looked real enough. And who was this bizarre eccentric man, this prosecutor asking for him to be locked up unless he paid the outrageously, obscenely huge amount of $145,000 x 10 which the leery judge had very kindly reduced to a measly $180,000 *cash*? Surely, this had all gone too far?

Vomit began to rise from his belly. *Up, up, up!* By sheer will, he closed the flap of cartilage at the root of his tongue and forced the puke back *down, down, down* to his alimentary canal.

It was always hardest after court, following the disappointment. Expectations building up for weeks as prayers are offered up. Hope on the cards. This could be it. Going home! Cherished thoughts of real food, the smell of a chip shop, an English pub, a Nigerian Buka. Then in a few minutes of acute torment, hope capriciously dashed. A new court date set. Depression returning vengefully accompanied by doubt. *Is there really a God?*

By the time Peter got back to Queensgate, they were flashing the news of his failure to reduce his bond virtually every hour on radio and television until even the most functionally illiterate American knew his heathen surname (as one guard put it). Fortunately, most inmates hadn't heard the news because there was no radio and they did not usually watch the lunch time news. They tended to congregate in the television area for the evening news. This was the moment Peter feared most.

He re-entered the cage, this hated zoo he prayed and hoped he would never see again. He collapsed onto his rack and wept. Hot tears of frustration and humiliation and anger and despair and fury rolled down his face, drenching his pillow and shirt. He was back where he started. Finished! Fucked!

Almost, because as always his sister Priscilla would not allow him to think that way. "The way to win is to keep your faith", she said, in her slightly stammered voice that never failed to stir the greatest inspiration in Peter. "God is only testing you to see what you are made of because he has great plans for you. Bleed a little then pick yourself up and prepare to fight again".

Peter was close to tears. It had been a difficult day. Hope deferred once again!

———

Peter willed his spirit to rise up from the condition of self-pity and doubt that was wearing him down. He opened his Bible and repeatedly read the words of the psalmist. *Lord, I pray to you. May this be the time you show me your favour!* He prayed to God to embrace him, not to allow his heart to grow faint. *I am tired Lord! I want an end to this.*

He must have heard Peter because the young cocky CO who had made the joke about "National Deadbeat Day" suddenly decided to do something unusual. After supper around 5.15pm, when most people normally headed for the TV area, he ordered everyone to go to their racks for a spot check. Apparently, it had come to his knowledge that some people had more than the stipulated number of bed sheets, pillowcases and uniforms, which was two of each and he was determined to catch the culprits.

The exercise took about twenty minutes. Then, to groans and soft curses, he gave everyone 30 minutes to clean up their living areas and prepare for inspection. The whole thing lasted about an hour, by which time the evening news had ended.

Peter breathed a grateful sigh of relief. But he knew it wasn't over and worse was to come. By morning, the newspapers would provide more ammunition for those who wanted to cut his heart out. He braced himself for the backlash.

The next morning, the headlines with his photo next to it looked fiercely and oppressively and disagreeably at him from every Cincinnati newspaper. He thought, this is the worst thing in the world. Groups of inmates huddled together gossiping about him. He knew because some snickered and glared while others regarded him with awe as he walked past.

By the middle of the day, the story had grown elaborate wings. As far as the story tellers were concerned, Peter was not only the worst dead beat dad, he had also become the most wanted man and -- get this -- the most *dangerous* man in Ohio, which was why the judge had refused to reduce his bond. Legends grew up around him. He was the black Jack the Ripper from England. He had successfully eluded the FBI and the CIA for over thirteen years, entering America under various guises. Even the Prosecutors office joined in the fiendish plot, describing in a television interview later that day how as part of the *Drop the Debt* campaign, Peter sneaked in and out of the country during the Seattle riots and hid from the FBI who were actively looking for him.

The story was a ridiculous exaggeration to the point of absurdity. First of all, Peter was not in the US during the Seattle riots, having left the campaign by the time it took place in early 2000. He visited America as part of a delegation a few months before the riots at the invitation of the American Treasury Secretary, Larry Summers. They held a meeting in his office to discuss how Washington could help alleviate third world debt and assist African countries in recovering monies stolen by their rulers and stashed in foreign banks. Peter had to be cleared by the FBI to be allowed into his office. Prior to that he had visited the White House as a news correspondent. So how could the FBI have been looking for him when they were the ones granting him passes into some of the most security conscious offices in the world?

It was easy to put these stories to a population -- especially those in jail -- used to being fed information without the benefit of objective analysis. Many inmates for instance couldn't read and those who could twisted the story beyond recognition. To Peter, their lies became like blows from hammers, raining down on him spitefully, each blow calculated to wreak maximum damage and weaken his resistance, completing the image of him as a monster who should be locked up and the keys thrown away. Peter heard the blows from those hammers from hell as if they were in his head and in his heart. It was a terrifying experience.

That the Chief Prosecutor could degenerate to such crude tactics, such shocking malevolence in order to build a case against him was unpardonably repellent. Peter tried to psychoanalyse him, coming up with various theories about how his unconscious mind worked. It was important for Peter to understand what kind of human being he was. What unspeakably primal drives and urges had this prosecutor man sublimated and which were now directing his actions? What conflicts and failings and guilt feelings and desires and unhappiness and unresolved disorders during his childhood lay suppressed and were now manifesting themselves through his neuroses and utter odiousness? How deep would one have to dig into his mind to uncover the *pathogenic moment,* the key to his sick, ill - bred, lying, egotistical, vengeful, spiteful, hate-driven impulse? What dark latent secrets lurked intimate, uncovered and unmasked? *Why have you come into my life?*

Peter thought that if he could somehow tunnel deep enough, perhaps he could unearth the prosecutors' traumas and parapraxes and help him get rid of them, restore his humanity and spirituality, regulate his ego complex. Maybe he didn't have any playmates when he was growing up. Perhaps he was projecting, characterising Peter as a monster when he was really the one. A man who hated children! What was he planning? How was he going to deliver the masterstroke, the coup de grace?

It had become clear to Peter in his immediate surroundings that after each televised court appearance and newspaper headline there would be a backlash. So he began to disguise himself as best as he could which, under the circumstances, consisted of taking off his glasses whenever he went into the chow hall or for outside recreation. In reality it wasn't much given that he was after all in an open jail where you couldn't hide. But at least it worked outside his floor where many inmates had heard about or seen him on the telly but still had difficulty recognising him in person.

However, Peter's cover was often blown when some kid or other on his floor would excitedly blurt out "I seen you on TV", to the hearing of everyone, as if he was some kind of hero. Even the guards often joined in with whoops of excitement and congratulatory pats on Peter's back -- such was their child like fascination with all things on television, especially *foreign* things on television. Discretion, subtlety, refinement were words which, try as he might, he simply could not associate with the average guard or inmate.

One particular inmate on Peter's floor was taking the piss.

"Hey mate", he mimicked in a poor English accent, to derisive laughter and encouragement from his chums. "Bloody TV star, with crumpets and tea and lots of dosh and bosh".

Peter lost it. "Why can't you bloody well grow up?" he snarled.

The inmate snarled back in American.

"Fuck you, deadbeat motherfucker".

The Tannoy crackled into life. "Quiet time, quiet time!" Peter seized the opportunity to slip away from the trenches.

Back in his corner, Peter fell on his knees. He had to get out. He had no idea how long the case might drag on, gobbling up thousands of dollars and trailing his entrails, *my damaged goods, my balls hanging out there for all to see,* in its wake. No matter how hard he tried to adapt, he knew he would never get over those massive anxiety attacks unless he got out quickly. It was the not knowing that made it worse, frayed the nerves. The wheels of justice moved desperately slowly and somehow Peter could not convey the urgency of his situation to Dobson, who suddenly seemed as if he always had some other over riding priority besides Peter.

"Lawyers, liars, lawyers", Reid intoned ponderously, heaving a fat sigh. "They see us as mere abstractions, as tools for their work. They can't tell me they really care about their clients. All they care about is money. They try to distil human experience into abstractions. They care shitless about you. Just yesterday my lawyer rushed up to me like a pre-programmed machine. ' "I got it down to six years" ' he bleats excitedly. Another abstraction! What about the individual, me, who has to serve those six years -- minute by excruciating minute, hour by hour, day by day, month after month?"

Reid's grievance made sense but it didn't offer a way out for Peter. Somehow he had to get Dobson to persuade the judge to get him out of that nick. But he couldn't figure out how. He had enough trouble just tracking down his eminence, his *paid* counsel. When he eventually did -- usually on the telephone -- Peter would pour out his thoughts. Dobson would listen with what seemed like patronising patience until the phones, which had a time limit of about twenty minutes would irritatingly cut Peter off in mid sentence just when he felt he was beginning to elicit much-needed sympathy.

But Dobson always had a sound plan of action although Peter didn't know it at the time.

The phones, Peter's only link to the outside world, soon became less friendly after he discovered they could not be trusted.   It was only a vague suspicion at first but the constant clicking noises on the line soon convinced him someone was listening in. In fact as he later discovered, not only where they listening, they were taping and monitoring all his calls.

How unfair the system was. They could detain him, tape his phone conversations, use anything he said against him and he could not do the same against them. He, the innocent one until proven guilty, could not listen to their conversations and know what evil plans they were hatching for his destruction. If he could not even rely on the phones, what else could he do?

Over the next few weeks, Peter's faith started to come alive. He was awed by St Paul's epiphany -- the manner in which he was struck to the ground in a blinding peak experience and forced to see God. Something similar but not quite as dramatic appeared to be happening to him. He realised he'd been ignoring the spiritual side of his life. In the past, he had failed to make His acquaintance. How empty his life had been. How full it would become if only he could push doubts away and allow His everlasting sun to shine its perpetual light in his life.

But though Peter was more inclined to open up to Him in the circumstances, he still hesitated because not only did he continue to feel doubt... *how could You exist in absolute perfection, yet create men and women who are far from perfect and force them to run the risk of eternal damnation...* he felt a bit like a hypocrite, calling on Him only because he needed help.

21

PETER'S TRIAL DATE WAS set for July 17th.

"Definitely trial by jury!" Dobson hissed when in court Peter was asked to choose between a judge and jury. Dobson belonged to that group of lawyers, and there were quite a few of them, that regarded bench trials with extreme repugnance. Lawyers who always defend and never prosecute! To the likes of Dobson, the jury was the "great equalizer" where ordinary people could hope to obtain justice against the powerful. Dobson was pretty sure a judge in that Republican dominated mid west town would almost certainly bury Peter. "The judge is a politician. He will be hard to predict, but most likely will not be independent", Dobson whispered to Peter.

Peter hesitated. His instinct was to waive his right to a jury and opt for a bench trial. It was born of years growing up under the formidable shadow of his father, a respected Supreme Court Justice in Nigeria, considered by many to be experienced, fair and impartial. Surely his interests would be better served by such wise and tempered jurists as Dad, Peter reasoned.

But after Dobson reminded Peter that, unlike their Nigerian or British counterparts, judges in America have traditionally always been in the political spotlight, canvassing for votes and funds, that both the judge and the chief prosecutor on Peter's case were politicians elected on the Republican ticket and that in fact the chief prosecutor was the local chieftain of the Republican Party, Peter agreed wholeheartedly to a jury trial. The stage was set for a clash of the titans – Peter's lawyer Dobson and the Prosecutors office. Who would come out top dog?

22

SLOWLY BUT OPPRESSIVELY CONSTANT, the days rolled on. Peter had over a month of waiting before his next court appearance. The hardest thing with doing *dead* time was the not knowing whether they were going to find one guilty and what, in the interim they could do with or *to* one. Would they, *could* they plant some drug in his locker and slap another charge on him if only to damage him further? Could they harm him physically, break his body as well as his spirit?

Peter tried to keep himself as busy as he could. *An idle mind is the devil's workshop!* One could believe that the chief spirit of evil was already working overtime in that jail, with its herds of brutish, undeveloped minds and unbalanced lives, and Peter wasn't going to add himself to the list. *Old Nick,* if indeed he existed, had succeeded in turning many into unthinking animals with sense organs and nervous systems -- carnal carrots able to respond dangerously and rapidly to stimuli, but unable to exercise their minds positively.

Peter read a variety of books. When he tired of them, he

turned to writing down his thoughts and observations. Then he interviewed any inmate he could get a hold of -- even the guards spent quite a bit of time with him. He became a sort of father confessor to everyone who had a real or fancied grievance or cause for complaint against the system. People -- guards and inmates alike -- regularly came to his corner to whinge and moan to their hearts content while he furiously took notes. From their peevish grumblings and whining complaints, Peter learnt that several of the officers were themselves victims of broken relationships from which dependents had emerged and that they were preyed upon by the child support system. Those who wanted other careers were not allowed to change jobs because the system feared any break might prevent them from meeting the outrageously high support payments they were being forced to make.

A new day dawned. Peter killed time, a captive in confinement. In a cell! *Caged!* An animal in a zoo! In shock! Stunned! Confused! Frightened! Depleted! Broken! A captive in a lost world, living half a life! The triumph of the Prosecutor ahead of November's ballot!

Peter slept. Not because he was tired, but because, as all in-mates knew, sleep was another way of killing time and cheating the county out of doing real time. The problem was that lots of sleep also meant that he ended up staying awake for much longer.

"Maybe they should employ cryogenics," Reid said, during one of his merry moments. "Freeze the inmates until their time is over. For a county so obsessed with and hungry for money, the process of freezing would actually be cheaper for them".

Late at night or during "quiet time" or early in the morning, stultifying boredom and uncertainty overshadowed Peter like a storm cloud, closing out all positive thoughts, stripping him of comfort, leaving him sad, lonely and forlorn. Living became a struggle, filled with dread, something to look forward to with great apprehension, or shrink from.

The clock crawled. Could he live through another day of this? How could he survive another second in here? How much longer could he endure this seismic emotional disturbance, this earthquake size trauma? What would he do if things failed to go his way?

Through the barred windows -- and he spent as much time as he was allowed there -- Peter stared at the hills of Kentucky, the bridge over the Ohio River. Other times, he kept to himself, eating little, tossing about restlessly on his narrow rack, wallowing in unrestrained misery, among his misfortunes.

My dearest Jul, I am bereft without you. Capricious fate has forced me to re-enter this den of doom, this house of horrors, this cold unyielding place of concrete walls and barred windows and locked gates. I cannot foretell, much as I'd like to, when my power of self-determination will be restored, when my slave status will be revoked, when my liberty will come. I am in a surreal purgatory, a state of mind where I can no longer perceive reality properly -- like a series of pictures and events in the mind of a sleeping person, glimpses of reality revealed through shrouded parables, as if the sun is slowly risen over patches of darkness and its uneven light has removed some illusions...

Mid-afternoon. Peter laid down on his rack. The television was pumping out pictures of the war in Palestine. This particular round of violence spared no one, neither Israeli nor Arab children. For both, as Peter knew only too well, the horrors of war had become real and damaging, physically and psychologically. Traumatised by injury and the experience of unthinkable atrocities, the pictures showed fearful eyes, full of sorrow and panic. One pre-school child, witness to brutality, weeping uncontrollably into the camera, clearly expecting his dead parents, murdered before his eyes by rocket fire, to return.

Peter's vision blurred, the TV report forcing his bored, tormented mind to scan the years and rest on the ghosts of 1967 to 1970. It was the one period he did not want to think about because of the nightmare that he knew came with it. His head began to pound. To have known the particularly brutal effects of war as a child, such macabre horror at seven! He had been one of the so-called "resilient" ones as the psychologists put it, those children who had lived through situations of extreme danger, anxiety and insecurity and had not only managed to survive but to show remarkable recoverability. Well to some extent, because now that he was much older and better educated about such things, Peter knew that some of his reckless anti-social behaviour as a young school lad and his extreme sensitivity to death and harm as a grown up were two of the common symptoms.

The third and most frightening diagnostic was his mental capacity to retain and revive events and images, to draw the monster back from memory.

Peter shrank from the recollection in dread. But it had already entered, the mental images strikingly bright, clearly perceptible.

1967. Seven - year old Peter, sat in class at prep school listening to the Canadian teacher Miss Ray droning on. His thoughts were focused not on her but on the period afterwards when he would get home, swap his school uniform for jeans and T-shirt and go into the valley with his chums. There had been rumours that a family of chimps had escaped from the zoo and where sheltering in some bushes near the bottom of the valley where the footpath ended in a flat riverbed. Zoo officials were planning to lay a trap to capture them. "They had better do it quickly", Miss Ray had said with a snort when the story broke a day earlier. "Otherwise they'll soon end up on the dinner tables of straggling villagers". Most kids in school were planning to be there to witness the capture, Peter among them.

Just after three in the afternoon, the end of the school day. Under grey skies, the pupils trooped into the courtyard and out the gate to the busy main road, heading towards the valley. Then suddenly, what was that whistling noise coming from above? Peter, jostling through the crowd, hearing it and looking up. Seconds later, a formation of Mig fighters and Ilyushin bombers, bursting through the clouds, flying low. It was the first attack aircraft the kids had ever observed and seeing them in perfect formation, most reacted as if they were at an air show. They waved and cheered as the planes broke formation, with several children, running towards the approaching aircraft.

Then without warning, the planes suddenly bearing down on them, their gun turrets blazing. Large objects tumbling out of their bellies towards the ground. One of the bombs crashing directly onto the roof of the school, killing fifteen students and three teachers instantly, maiming and wounding dozens more. The kids scattering in panic, Peter running with them, hearing another deafening bang, feeling his feet lift off the ground, his body tossed like a rag doll into a collapsed roadside stall. Then more loud explosions, the sound of tearing metal, the screams of the wounded, the gurgling sounds of the dying, the pools of blood, the disembodied parts, that severed, twitching hand still wrapped around a dollop of mashed cassava, the blackened torso belonging to that lanky ten-year old, soft-spoken boy…the body without a head…

Loud ringing noises, rousing Peter from his macabre reveries. It was the fire alarm drill. Oozing sweat, Peter staggered out of his rack, down the flights of stairs and into the courtyard, along with the rest of the inmates. They marched twice around the courtyard and then dutifully trooped back to their various floors.

The exercise temporarily cleared Peter's mind of the horrors of war. He lay down on his rack and looked out the window. Up above, a detachment of birds flew past. He could sense they were squawking loudly, although he could not hear them from behind the sealed, barred windows. He remembered some book he'd read recently – one of a series he used to kill time – marvelling at the clearly defined flight path that birds seemed to follow. How did they know where to go? Who showed them the route? How did they do it? The author had no idea and neither did Peter. But *something* was impelling them. Was there a Platonic "idea" bird behind them? Or were they born with innate flight plans and merely waited for their bodies and wings to grow strong enough before they could actualise it, the author speculated quite intelligently, Peter thought?

Peter, the horrors of war temporarily relegated, continued to watch the squadron of birds, fascinated, until they disappeared over the sloping hills and fringe of trees.

23

It took a while before inmates stopped harassing and demonising Peter but by then he had gone past caring and no longer exhibited any outward fear, although he still quaked inside. Many more had begun to respect him, though they still found him foreign and strange, or perhaps because of it. Peter had to admit that on the whole life had improved and he wasn't attracting as much hostility any more. He was a British Nigerian in *their* nick who kept pretty much to himself and for bizarre reasons they couldn't comprehend, preferred to stick his nose in a book rather than sit out in the lounge area gambling or passively watching television like everyone else.

Others though still found Peter utterly baffling. *Who da fuck you think you is punk ass mo'fucker?* His "accent" and the coverage of his case by the media made it clear to them that he certainly didn't come from their neck of the globe. His world, the places he had lived and visited, too numerous to recall except for the big ones, were far beyond them – Paris, Monte Carlo, London, Rome, Lagos, Accra, Brisbane, Sydney, Tokyo, Havana, Kingston,

Bangkok...sigh! *Bangkok...Memories of hedonistic holidays...*
Well, tough shit, punk ass! Cos' you in New Jack City now mother-
fucker! Das right! You is in da hood!
To them Peter seemed terribly aloof but also rather cool.
Indifferently, impudently cool! Peter on the other hand couldn't
stand the way they barged in on his private moments just to hear
"that accent" and he did not hesitate to make it plain to them,
sometimes by snapping at the offender.

Peter would be engrossed in a book. Suddenly his thoughts
would be savagely interrupted by some bloke entering his corner
uninvited.

"Whatcha readin' England?" he would practically shout into
Peter's ear.

Peter would look up into the face of a complete stranger standing there, staring quizzically at him.   Such...such...utterly grace-
less intrusion!

"For God's sake man, haven't you got any bloody manners?"
would come Peter's angry response.   "Cant you even say excuse
me?"

The culprit would slink away, shocked by his vehemence.

Sometimes Peter felt for them.   One fellow who had been arrested in Florida while he was still high on some unnamed but
hugely potent drug floated around for days on a crest of absolute
need.   He approached Peter's corner looking glazed.

"Hey England, you got anything to eat?"

Peter looked up at him and something in his slurred speech
evoked pity rather than the usual hostility.

"What the devil's the matter with you, mate?"

"I took some pills in Miami before my arrest and I think they're
still working", he said.

"Well, what was it?" Peter asked.

"I don't know", came the reply.   "I stole someone's
prescription".

Peter shook his head in disgust and handed him a packet of
crisps. The fellow like the rest of them lived in a child like world

of make belief dominated by television and movies -- a dream like state of restlessness and boredom where all that mattered was the unbridled pursuit of Epicurean mores, a life predicated on the maximisation of pleasure. Since reading and writing required application -- a bit of a bother -- they were to be studiously avoided.

The lull in hostilities mattered little. Peter desperately wanted to get out of there. One way out of the quagmire was to negotiate a deal. But Dobson was not keen on it. Against his advice, Peter's family decided to approach the prosecution for a possible settlement that would serve both parties. This was not an admission of guilt. Just fear that with so much publicity, they might never find an unbiased jury. The idea of being sent to the state penitentiary, a *convict,* was something no one, least of all Peter himself, wanted to contemplate. On the other hand, he wasn't going to plead guilty. How could he when they were the ones who were assaulting him?

The offer was made privately through Dobson's office, after what they perceived to be positive discussions had taken place between Peter's brother, Chu and the *woman.*

The crude disdainful response came in a brief telephone call from the Chief Prosecutors office.

"You can take your laughable offer and shove it".

That left the family in no doubt that the prosecutor's office meant business and had every intention of "frying your ass like an omelette", as Reid put it. The horrible possibility of at least two years in the state penitentiary stared Peter boldly in the face. Not only did they callously reject the offer, they gave the story to the newspaper with the highest circulation, which published it immediately, writing it up in such a way as to make Peter appear to be incontrovertibly guilty. They included a quote from the *woman* ridiculing the offer, which she had appeared to accept earlier. (It became clear why a few days later when she demanded a pay-off of tens of thousands of dollars). Much of Peter's side of the story, which had been given to the same paper in an interview with Chu, his brother, was ignored.

Peter was crushed. For most of the afternoon, he lay awake on his rack, driven by a feeling of tremendous insecurity. Why hadn't he listened to Dobson's advice? He knew he had to try and put it behind him and look forward, as his sister Priscilla suggested. But how could he when he knew there was more to come in a couple of hours on the evening television news, which would surely have picked up the story. They would right now be sharpening their knives, embellishing the story, raising the stakes against him, pointing their daggers at his heart, doing him incredible damage. As if they hadn't caused enough mischief already!

24

4ᵀᴴ ᴏꜰ Jᴜʟʏ ᴀʀʀɪᴠᴇᴅ! But the bell that was ringing at Queensgate on America's Independence Day was not the bell of freedom, as far as Peter was concerned. It was a deep, hollow, metal gong tolling with oppression and injustice, sounding loud and clear to remind him he was locked up at their pleasure. It rang to force him to wake up and obey their rules. There was no statue of liberty here, no blindfolded lady holding freedom's torch high. Instead, he was yoked down by the weight of tyranny, yearning to breathe free. The towering monument did not symbolise freedom. It stood for enslavement. To him it said: "Give me your free, your honest and your just and I will enslave and crush them afoot".

She was certainly not his statue of liberty for it was here under her watchful gaze that her minions imprisoned his body, that he was persecuted by the prosecutor, locked down, imposed upon, broken. The talented, destructive life and times of Peter Oti! The incredible meteoric rise and the horrendous manipulated spectre of the fall of Peter the star.

Peter looked back at his last two months in captivity, his seismic shock. They had been the hardest in recent memory. He had endured a lot, sometimes with remarkable patience, other times with extreme restlessness and hopelessness. Delays, postponements, continuances, waiting to go to court, waiting to see the judge, waiting to see his lawyer. Waiting, waiting, waiting!

He still had several weeks as a captive before his trial and a lot longer if heaven forbid he was to be found guilty. As Dobson said, this was not just a case of child support. It was a political case with major implications!

Peter prayed to God with all his heart. *Look with favour upon me O Lord and if it is Your Will, grant me my freedom and my life back.* Peter believed with all his soul that he was fighting a just war. His appeal for a settlement had been thrown back in his face. The battle lines were drawn. There was only one way left now for things to be settled: fight.

"The tape is within sight", Dobson said with characteristic flair. "But we need extra effort and vigilance to breast it".

The enemy was also within sight. Dobson could not afford to be taken by surprise. He had to be fully aware of Peter's defence defects, where the case showed signs of being porous. It was time to play political *ju-jitsu*, taking weaknesses and turning them into strengths, cleverly using the throws and blows of Peter's attackers to disable them.

The political gains for the victorious would be immense. For the defeated, the losses would be considerable. It could mean political damage for the Chief Prosecutor, loss of freedom and career for Peter and loss of face and money plus a possible charge of perjury for the *woman.*

Peter started taking stock of his situation. Every day, he pored over his files that Dobson or one of his aides brought over, looking over every shred of evidence for and against him, for-seeing every possibility, anticipating questions, answers, angles. Dobson was his coach and guide.

"There can be no mistakes", he said. "We can't afford any screw-ups".

Peter read the transcript again. The deliberate attempt to deceive the court, the imposture, made him shiver. Did no one bother to check, to verify her outrageous claims? Her statement was on public record and the politicians had ensured its survival, using it for their political smear campaign without bothering to check its authenticity.

On the point of law, the vital question was whether Peter should have obeyed a court order that was in fact not based on truth but on falsehood told under oath. Peter and Dobson went over that point of law over and over again.

"There was no way I could have", Peter told him. "Compliance would have implied agreement which in turn would have implied truth. If a traffic warden gives you a $500 parking ticket in a $20 zone for an offence you were wrongly accused of committing, do you pay it or protest against it? I did what I believe I should have done -- filed an objection and waited for a response that never came".

25

Peter rolled over on his rack and groaned dismally. What he had originally intended as a roar of wrath could only manage to come out as a feeble, dreary, miserable, inept sob loaded with grief. It was the only way he could express the darkness of feelings that lay on him like a pall of black velvet.

He had lost track of time. He had not the remotest idea what time or day it was. He could of course look up to the clock on the wall. But the hapless British Nigerian could not will himself to look up. How long he had been lying like that Peter did not know. It could have been centuries, but what difference would it make?

It was the waiting that got to him, filling him with intractable dread, black as a hat. Anticipation burned in him, turning the waiting into sheer agony. He dared not do anything else but wait for fear it may make the waiting appear even longer.

Peter lay on his rack, his back leaning slightly on the metal headboard, and waited some more. There was nothing for him to do but sit it out.

As the minutes and hours of his apocalypse dragged on, Peter's mind threaded its way through the thicket, plunging into a dark wood, stumbling into trees, bumping into roots, tearing through bushes, gasping for breath, heedless of scratches, images of war, returning with a vengeance, tormenting him.

The Irish priest and the Irish nun in the little village church near Owerri, sheltering some of their flock from advancing, rampaging federal forces -- a wounded Biafran soldier using a crude log as a walking stick, along with his wife and two children aged five and one respectively and a new born baby less than three days old. The Irish priest, old and gaunt, the Mom and baby, in poor health. Some thirty federal soldiers, part of the dreaded Third Marine Commandoes, known for their brutality, suddenly bursting into the churchyard, opening fire, cutting down the wounded soldier instantly, then lining up the priest, the nun, the Mom and the five year old against the mud wall and shooting each one between the eyes. Afterwards, according to one refugee who watched the whole thing hidden, they placed the baby in the arms of the screaming one year old, with the bodies of their parents and sibling, as well as the priest and nun lying next to them…A week later, Biafran forces who had recaptured parts of Owerri found them and took photographs. Peter remembered the pictures: the one year old, having abandoned the baby, lying in the rotting arms of his dead mother…

Peter puffed and blew, forcing his mind back to reality with a thud. He could not see where he was going. His wind, already a little short, was failing him fast. *The man is after me. I can hear him and every minute I am dreading being clutched from behind.*

What will he be in a thousand years? What will the prosecutor be? What will the *woman* be? Would there be any difference between them? Or would they be nothing more than insignificant atoms that had sub-divided into neutrons and protons and electrons? Forgotten excrescences that once bubbled up to the surface of the earth and then vanished? What would it matter? Nothing! No meaning in a cosmic context!

Peter crawled out of the hawthorns. Soon the dark woods

would return and swallow him up, once more and onward he would drag his weary mind, winding among dark bushes and bewildering trees and shadowy thickets.

Peter watched the birds in flight and he made up his mind never to cage an animal again. No visits to environmentally unsafe zoos -- ever. He could well imagine what zoo animals were going through. Stuck in a small cell, condemned to a life of imprisonment until death. Peter was in for a couple of months and almost lost it, what more they.

26

End of the first week of July!

The first time, Peter saw him instinctively before they met. To be accurate, Peter sensed rather than saw his presence. There was something about him, as if he had always been there unseen long before they met, immovable, like an invisible rock.

Peter was lying on his rack, scanning the pages of a book on astronomy. *Point zero…that moment fifteen million years ago when all visible matter condensed in a single point at an inconceivable temperature…In five billion years, our sun will run out of nuclear fuel and die…*

Suddenly Peter's heart began to beat faster. His hands trembled violently. His head was in turmoil, his mind in a whirl.

Foresight! Hindsight! Insight! Sixth sense! he heard or rather felt someone say.

Peter looked up and saw a man sitting on the rack opposite his. He had never seen him before and had no idea when he came in.

He was staring at Peter steadily but there was nothing disconcerting about his gaze. He had a gentle face and the beginnings of a kindly smile hovered around the corners of his mouth. He gave Peter a genial nod. It was difficult to guess his age. He reminded Peter of a wizard or a very patient, wise man, at once young and old. Or perhaps he was a ghost!

He asked no questions but Peter could feel without conscious intention, intuitively, that he understood and was ready and willing to speak to him, to answer whatever questions he might have. He felt as if a massive current of electricity was making a rushing attack up his spine.

Good morning brother!

Again, Peter felt rather than heard him say the words. Such things didn't …there had to be some rational…

There was a tremendous crash and the sound of rushing water, startling Peter out of the meditation trance into which he supposed he had fallen. For a moment or two he wondered where he was and whether he was in a dream.

Peter looked down and saw the shattered shards of a large plastic water container at the foot of his rack and water all over his corner. He looked up and saw Biter the crime boss sitting on the bed across, glowering at him. He reminded Peter of a coiled rattlesnake. Two others who looked like pirates sat next to him, smiling menacingly at Peter. Neither they nor Biter seemed to notice the stranger who was sitting opposite Peter, on his corner mates rack. Or if they did, they simply chose to ignore him.

"Yo, British punk ass mo'fucker ", said Biter looking at Peter and cocking his head to one side impudently. His fellow degenerate gang members laughed rowdily.

"You thought we'd forgotten about you, didn' ya? Thought you was just gon' slip out and slide away". Biter stands and does a short moonwalk. His dissolute chums applaud.

"Wachoo gat in dat locker, boy? I'm starvin'".

Peter didn't answer. Nor did he move any part of his body. But he cast his eyes around wildly like a frightened animal.

The crime boss moved a few paces down the side of his rack, his nostrils flaring at the prospect of drawing blood. Utterly primitive! His eyes were blazing with deep malevolence, full of the brute power that ruled in that animal den. He casually raised his mattress and pulled out a long wooden stick that had been sharpened to a point like a spear.

It was 7pm. Dinner was over and most inmates, including Reid, were gathered in the adjoining pod room either playing card games or watching television in the viewing area. Else they were queuing up at the other end for the five telephones that could be used for collect calls only. Tucked away in the corner a few were attending Bible classes. The guards were sitting in the middle of the pod room, miles away from Peter's rack, playing cards.

All this information raced through Peter's consciousness in little more than three seconds. He was dreadfully aware that there was no one near enough to see what was going on. If anything happened, he would have no help. Biter had chosen his moment. The thought made Peter's blood run cold. He suddenly felt horribly fragile and vulnerable.

Something in his anxiety racked mind told him he should not appear to be frightened, must not surrender to fear. So with cold perspiration trickling down his face, Peter lay there and waited. His glasses lay aslant on his nose. He was gripped by one urgent thought: how could he evade this imminent threat, beat a retreat from this fast approaching *like a freight train* nightmare?

Peter had always been a bit of a gym freak, but had resolutely refused to do any exercises since his incarceration. He had wanted his body to wither away and die. He was suddenly filled with deep regret for this blunder. At that moment, he wished his body had been healthier and more able to endure the physical punishment a frightening premonition now told him with horrible clarity lay ahead.

He had already started silently gurgling for air. He would have scrambled up and at least fled, but every ounce of breath was out of him now and he could not. He lay on that rack quite spent.

An abnormal silence seemed to envelop everything. The scene could have been a slow motion diorama as Biter came towards him, slowly, deliberately and menacingly. Peter cut his eyes this way and that, looking for a way out, a means of checking the steady advance of this phantasmagorical, compact lethal mass towards his rack side and his destruction, armed with a crude but rather effective looking weapon, intent on doing him unspeakable, perhaps even fatal harm.

Then the brute was standing over Peter smiling eerily.

"I said, watchoo gat in dat locker, boy?" he growled.

Peter's mind was in a whirl. *Got to do something or this bastard is really going to sweat me...but what?*

As if driven by some unseen force, Peter's eyes locked with those of the stranger sitting opposite. Suddenly he felt that charge of electricity rushing up his spine again. Energy, like fire, consuming him! A bright flash, filling his brain! Strength, coming to him mysteriously.

Biter was virtually upon him when Peter went into action. With a swing of his right arm, Peter sent him spinning. At the same time, his left arm flew to the spear, grabbing it with such speed and force, that the crime boss lost his grip and hit the wet ground with a startled squeak. A lightning bolt dropping from the ceiling could not have taken him more by surprise. Peter had come at him like a shot from the blue.

In a flash, Peter landed on Biter's shoulders, crumpling him. A startled sputtering yell escaped from his lips as he crumpled. Then Peter dropped his knees on the wiry back, pinning him down.

The crime boss wriggled like an eel, gasping and making anguished sounds. He struggled, but could not dislodge the knee that pinned him down. He twisted his head around to stare up at his unexpected assailant, his face filled with surprise, humiliation and yes, Peter noted with satisfaction, respect for he who had brought the *crime boss* to heel.

His two henchmen sat up slowly, stunned. Their eyes almost popping out at Peter, they slithered off, and in a few moments, disappeared from view.

Peter rocked, as the crime boss under him made a tremendous effort with his strong and sinewy body. For a long minute, the man fought, fiercely and savagely, then quite spent with his efforts, he collapsed back on the ground and lay panting and gasping for breath.

After that it was easy enough to hold him and Peter kept him pinned till a good couple of minutes had elapsed. Then he removed his knee and rose to his feet, holding the stick like a sword.

The crime boss staggered up, panting, looking as if he'd been dragged through a hedge backwards, his eyes smouldering at the British Nigerian. Suddenly he noticed the stranger sitting there and watching him coolly. For a moment or two it looked as if Biter would spring at either him or Peter but he seemed to think better of it. He gave Peter a weak scowl then made a movement to pass by his rack side. Peter stood like a rock in the way.

"No you don't!" Peter said coolly, moving a step nearer to the crime boss. "Get going and don't come back or you'll get very hurt".

The crime boss eyed him. For a moment he hesitated, then he turned around and slouched away in the direction of the pod room.

Peter watched him out of sight and slowly sat down. He let the stick drop to the ground. His hands were trembling, his head was throbbing and his legs felt weak. He could feel the electricity charge slowly draining out of his central nervous system. It sounded like the rush of a waterfall. He suddenly felt limp. He could hardly imagine the animal strength that had exploded from his body just a few minutes earlier. Was he dreaming or had he just witnessed the humiliation, reduction and – yes, *defeat* – Peter could allow himself that – of Biter the powerful crime boss? Had he Peter just set upon…was he the one who had just rush attacked and *reduced* the crime boss? Stunned him?

He turned towards his corner mate's rack to thank the stranger. But he was nowhere in sight.

27

THE NEXT TIME PETER saw the stranger was on July 12, less than eight days before his trial was due to begin. Peter had all but forgotten the incident with Biter the crime boss. It was almost as if it hadn't happened and Peter would have believed he dreamed it all if it hadn't been for the fact that Reid constantly reminded him that he hadn't heard a pip from Biter or any of his thugs since that fateful evening.

On this day, mid-morning, Reid was away meeting his attorney and Peter had been staring at the ceiling. As usual, he slept and woke up. The clock crawled and his heart palpitated. He slept some more. Thoughts mutated and decayed.

He awoke and drifted for a while, listening to shouts from inmates rushing to the window to gawk at something. David's dreadlocks flew through the air. The birdman hopped past. A fly hovered and then disappeared. Peter coasted.

Then he decided to write a letter to Juliet.

Hi Sweety… Nothing doing. Emptiness. Just waiting. Waiting in limbo. Waiting hopefully. Time passages. Passing time. Dead time. Empty time. Hopeful time.

After he sealed the letter and dropped it in the post box, Peter opened his book on astronomy.

The sun is about three million kilometres away…Its rays travel for eight minutes before they reach us…

Then he heard the voice and saw the face in his mind's eye.

"Did you know that the sun is just one of billions of other stars in our Galaxy – some of them are more than fifty thousand light years away from us? That means, Peter, that when we look at a star, we are looking fifty thousand years back in time. So the star may have already ceased to exist. If there were people there and they were looking at us, they'd be seeing primitive man or dinosaurs". The voice added softly: "Perhaps even Jesus performing miracles, or the Buddha in meditation".

Did the prosecutor ever think about that, Peter pondered in his reveries? Did he think about gravity and inertia? Does he know that we are nothing more than stardust unto which we shall all someday return? Does he know we are all part of the same universe, made of the same substance? Does he concern himself with the big questions that continue to weave a web of mystery? Where did he come from? What was his purpose? Why did he come into existence? If he knew all this, how could he be the person that he now was, nursing the callousness and heartlessness he now had?

"It actually helps us to look back in time Peter", the voice continued. "Because therein perhaps lies the key to the answers of how our universe developed. Because if every time we look up we are looking back possibly billions of years into the origins of the Galaxy, soon we would know exactly how we came into existence".

It was when I, Peter, couldn't answer those questions, Mr Persecutor, that I decided to write a book and fix you in it. I wanted so much to subdue and conquer you, to be able to manipulate and control you too, just as you had tried to do with me.

"The difference" said the voice of the stranger, reading his mind, "is that where he failed, you will succeed".

Suddenly there he was. A tall silhouette appearing silently, sitting on the same rack as before. A guardian angel arriving just in the nick of time to rescue him? Perhaps an alien from another planet? Somehow, Peter was not afraid.

"Good evening brother!" the stranger said in a deep voice. "How do you say in Nigeria: a man who pays respect to the great paves the way for his own greatness? Actually I think my favourite is this one: looking at a King's mouth one would think he never suckled at his mother's breast. It sounds so wise".

His name was Josh. Something about him seemed wondrous and other – worldly. His ears seemed rather long and strangely pinned back, like a Doberman pinscher in full flight. He was a strange enchanting creature and an incredibly good storyteller with a sharp eye for the most obscure detail and its significance. "I didn't get a chance to thank you the other day for helping me out of that rather awkward situation, although I'm not sure how", Peter said warmly.

Josh grinned. He got up and walked towards the barred windows and Peter followed. Outside the leaves were shining with rain that came down in a heavy downpour earlier.

"I didn't do anything. You did it all".

He reached over and patted Peter on the back.

"Good on yer mate!" he said, imitating an east London cockney accent.

Peter learned that Josh had been framed on a drugs charge ten years ago when he was thirty. Alone, stripped of everything and going crazy with despair, he prayed. He was sub-literate and could hardly read but to his amazement, he picked up the Bible and read it easily from cover to cover -- no problem. Then he read the Koran and the Bhagavad Gita and the writings of the Buddha. He prayed. He contemplated. He atoned -- a wronged man seeking the peace of God. The experience bound him to the

Holy Books forever. They became his shrine, a place he repaired to and renewed himself spiritually.

During the week they talked, Josh was like a mine of information on all things spiritual. There was always an answer, an explanation. He seemed to range with ease through the crannies of the metaphysical world, coming up with the most amazing and obscure facts, peppering them with humour and extraordinary insight.

"The devil is not ugly with horns, but is a most handsome angel. It is his wicked heart that makes him appear ugly".

He studied Peter's face.

"Satan came along and interrupted God's time table…"

Josh's eyes glowed like precious stones. Peter followed the direction of his voice and finger and stepped into a wonderland of giants and angels, spirits and saints, ghouls and devils in a way he had never experienced. Was this really the Bible, the book he had always found so boring? Yes indeed it was, Josh said. God's enchanted world. He had opened up a box full of sacred treasures that resonated with meaning and significance that had eluded Peter for years.

"Jesus was actually created by God. He was the first thing that the Father created -- the first Son of God, pre-eminent amongst the angels. The other sons of God are the angels, among them Lucifer, who was appointed by God as the guardian of the earth. That is why what he worships, we worship. He and his angels were floating up and down between heaven and earth and men thought of them as gods. They were the gods of mythology. They slept with daughters of men and gave birth to giants and "mighty men" like Hercules and malformed creatures with one eye, and so on. These angels were like Lucifer and God had warned them not to do what they were doing with men. But they continued sinning and doing monstrous things like having sex even with animals. That's why you had creatures like centaurs. They actually existed. People started worshipping these creatures as false gods. Satan had corrupted everything on the surface of the earth.

So God decided to destroy both man and beast. That's why the floods came because these bad angels inhabited men, women and animals, even trees to trick men into believing they were gods. Their offspring -- giants and malformed people and animals -- had to die in order for humanity to live. Then the bad angels were cast into the abyss. This was the part of Genesis that was lost, but there is just enough in Genesis 6 to help you understand what happened..."

He watched Peter's fascination and discovery with his dark, sparkling eyes, smiling to himself with undisguised almost child-like pleasure.

"God searched for a perfect person to save mankind. It took a perfect man -- Adam -- to sin and it had to take a perfect man to remove sin. God searched high and low to find this man. And eventually it fell on Jesus. This was why he had to be born without sin. He was placed in Mary because he had to be born of a woman in order to become flesh. In order to be able to judge flesh, he had to be flesh. He had to go through the cycle of 33 years before he died. 33 was the age of reason. There is no date for his birth because his birth was not significant. It was his death that mattered. Yet man gave him a birthday in December".

The tannoy crackled into life, announcing the start of two hours of outside rec. As they walked along the basketball court that was heaving with sweaty bodies, Josh suddenly asked Peter:

"Have you decided whether you are going back into your business again?"

"What business?"

"The business of broadcast journalism".

Peter was wrapped in his own thoughts for a while.

"After all of this? I don't know yet. "

Josh looked at him. "Well many people, myself included, are beginning to mistrust the media. Just look at what they've done to you, the play of words. No checking of facts, nothing! *How many killed?...*thirty...*make it more than sixty – that's a better figure...Wounded?...*About forty five...*say hundreds, it sounds better* *on air...How did he get here?... He came voluntarily...Say he was captured through the tenacious efforts of Hamilton County Prosecutors office... where did he arrive from...London, England...make it West Africa...say he was hiding in darkest West Africa where, using voodoo, he thought he could escape the long arm of US justice..."*

"Well you can't hold it against all media" Peter said defensively. "Some like the BBC World Service and CNN International are relatively objective. I just fell into the hands of the wrong kind".

"I feel sorry for the public", Josh continued, "aching for the truth, but not really sure they are getting it. Fifty years ago, abortion, murder, corruption, pornography would never have been tolerated. But you lot have seduced the world to change its attitudes and its tolerance levels. Why?"

"I'll tell you why", Josh continued in answer to his own question. "The world is in a tangle because we no longer pray. We have become more fascinated with television and have lost our wisdom to you journalists".

Peter nodded gravely as Josh went on.

"Well its work and you journos have to do what you are told, I suppose. Afterwards, when the seedy work is done, you lot appear at the pub down the road, drink yourself senseless and be shown the way home, having deadened your conscience and your nerves. Now that you've seen it from the victim's perspective and seen your erstwhile colleagues at work against you, is it a burden you want to carry any more? I would have thought that for you, P.R. work would be the logical thing. You could of course just try TV news again. They seemed like they really wanted you for a while there. Maybe they'll hold a position for you".

"Not jolly likely", said Peter. " I really don't think I matter that much to them. They'll all gossip about me for a while. *Isn't it terrible what happened to him? Pity, he had such talent...* News will continue to be covered and they'll find a new face to replace me. Give it a few months and they won't even remember who I am".

There was a pause as they strolled along. Then Josh said suddenly.

"Well then you should write a book.   Y'know, the Ultimate Over-Confessional Modern Rehab-Celebrity novel".

As he walked away he shouted over his shoulder:

"Make sure at the very least it tells some truths about the injustices of the justice system.   Let it be a merciless critique of something called America in which I once believed but which has sold its soul to the dollar and has become empty of compassion".

And that was the last Peter ever saw of him in the flesh.

One day, a note mysteriously appeared under Peter's pillow.

Dear Peter,

Your time at Queensgate will be short.   I already know this.   But I'm sure for you it will also seem exceedingly long.   Both are equally true.   When I was inside it was very long but looking back now in retrospect it was short.

Well, good luck with your book (I assume you are going ahead with it).   I'm sure that Queensgate and the Ham County justice system will continue to operate, indeed thrive, in spite of it.   But if you could in a small way remind people that they are the Power, not merely hapless victims, and to take back what is theirs in the true sense of democracy, then you would have achieved something great.   They cannot continue to simply shrug their shoulders for democracy can only find true expression in the preservation of the rights of the individual – rights that are manifested in their interaction with the institutions of democracy, such as the Judiciary.

As you can see dear Peter the current state of this judiciary is the mirror of a fractured democracy.   It arose out of a people's need for justice, just like all the other institutions, crystallising into one big democracy called America. But now all the institutions are sliding off, becoming more a reflection of themselves than of the people, the system alienating its creator.

Peter sat down on his rack.   Where had he read those very words? Such powerful words? Was it Kant or was it…Kiekergaard wasn't it? – Philosophy 101 – "*…an existential situation, a necessary pre-disposition to a higher spirituality…*" Yes, it was definitely Kiekergaard. "*…My inner need and despair must lead me to this* *peak experience, this final and decisive option, when I take the leap of faith into the arms of the living God..."*

Peter read on:

Now Peter, for our last lesson. Just like the law of gravity is inherent in nature -- what goes up must come down – the law of morality or conscience is inherent in our minds and souls, irrespective of whether we were born in India or the Middle East, The British Isles or the West African coast. This Peter is what I'd like to remind you of. To help refocus your attention on that which has always been there but which we have forced or relegated into dormancy through sin. Jesus, Mohammed, Buddha, Krishna – they all said pretty much the same things: the Kingdom is within you...self-conquest not the conquest of the many realms of the universe is valour supreme...love your neighbour as yourself...do not take advantage of or exploit your fellow human being...look inside for the answer lies within...From the inside outwards...So you must take time out to meditate Peter and you must do right by others.

It sounded suspiciously like Kant. How did this sub-literate man develop such writing skills? How did he encounter such profound philosophical thinking?

Once again Josh had anticipated his thoughts.

I didn't say it. God said it through the mouths and the writings of the prophets and philosophers. He just reveals it to me Peter and I believe it. Just like I believe in you. Try, in these years of the great jubilee, in this culture of death, amid desperate circumstances, try to find life Peter. Find yourself in an existential situation, find your soul, then leap into a higher spirituality. There you will always find me.

Love Josh

Peter stared at the words and wept!

28

Five days to go before the scheduled trial. Less than a week before possible freedom! In any case, five more days and the uncertainty would end.

Peter was counting the days. His brain was working overtime searching for ways out of his captivity, analysing potential difficulties, obstacles that could stand in the way, between him and the road he so yearned to tread, the road to freedom.

Peter and Dobson spent many hours together, mapping out a strategy. Dobson guiding and inspiring. At least now, with the spectre of Biter the crime boss behind him – Peter had long since stopped worrying about who was coming in front, behind or by his side – he could concentrate on the main task ahead.

In the end the plan which was in fact Dobson's plan was simple: keep them believing they had already won. They'll come unprepared.

Peter wasn't sure he bought it completely. To him it seemed terribly unrealistic – simplistic even -- to expect such naivety, such unpreparedness from a county prosecutor who was leading a case that was generating huge media interest. Dobson, his eyes gleaming, revealed he had already put the plan into action.

"I wrote to them a few days ago asking once again to meet to try and work out a deal. As expected they took the bait and wouldn't meet. Then a group led by your brother Zik went to see them to plead. But they wouldn't budge. I can see the chief prosecutor sitting around writing his victory speech for the evening TV news instead of preparing his case. You gotta trust me. I know these people and how they think. Besides, this is the only way you're gonna clear your name".

Peter swallowed hard and nodded. No one else, not even his family, knew of this strategy. He was paying Dobson a hefty retainer so he would have to trust him wouldn't he? There were no guarantees except money -- *up front if you please sir!* It didn't seem fair. But at least Peter could *hope* for justice because he had hired a lawyer who was a Pit Bull and who knew how to get into the trenches where the real fight was and who could take on the Teutonic establishment without fear. At least Peter could afford to hire him – well, he couldn't really afford to but in any case, there it was. Money in the bank! *Dobson's* bank! Enough to commend his fate into the hands of the Pit Bull!

What if he had been unable to hire another lawyer? What if he had been stuck with the cadaver? Peter shuddered! It didn't seem fair that only those who could afford it could hope for justice. It was definitely not fair that the poor should be the victims of rules set by the rich ruling classes who were far removed from their circumstances. It was an unjust system that preyed on the poor. Justice had to be for all not based on the amount of money one had. And, as Josh said, wasn't it the unspeakably poor conditions of work and pay imposed by the rich that often forced the poor to supplement their income by selling drugs and getting into prostitution and failing to pay fines that double after one week and child support and so on. Plus they'd have to find another thirty dollars to pay the government for their arrest. Clearly most people simply could not afford their outrageous fines so they ended up getting locked up. Not all cases of course but many cases, enough to raise serious questions.

As far as Peter was concerned, Ham County was like a big plantation and the conditions were similar to slavery. The difference was the year and the name had changed.

Imagine, as some philosopher Peter had read said, if those who made the laws suddenly had to change places with the victims of society. Perhaps society should require that people who make the law change places to properly evaluate the justice of the laws that are made, suggested the philosopher. That would be the day. Peter, absorbed, lay there, immersed in his musings.

29

Four days to go.

Peter received a surprise visit that greatly encouraged him.

"England, go to B stairwell. You have a professional visit" crackled the Tannoy.

It was Mick Bell, his old friend from Xavier University. Mick was quite a guy. Born and bred in Cincinnati, he was tall, blue eyed and blonde and used to cut quite a figure with the ladies at school. But now he was older and a little pudgier, but his face hadn't changed. Looking at him, Peter suspected he was still probably as incredibly well organised as he used to be at University.

Mick was now a lawyer and that was why Peter had been told he had a professional visit. He was married to another lawyer Karen, who took on complex divorce cases.

Mick beamed when he saw Peter.

"It's good to see you old buddy".

Peter's spirit lifted a few notches. "Same here" he replied.

They both started laughing. They drew close and embraced.

Then Mick stepped back and looked Peter up and down with a worried expression on his face. "Karen's offering her services to you free, Peter. We're in the battlefield together, buddy. The bullets are flying and were gonna draw some blood. But we're gonna win. I'm not even gonna ask you what's it like in here or how its been with that shameful media circus. I just want you to know Karen and me are going to do our best".

Waves of deep intense gratitude washed over Peter. A friend indeed! Peter's hands were shaking terribly as Mick said goodbye.

30

THREE DAYS TO GO.

Three days before Peter would have to face the full final circus. Sink or swim. God, how he hated this place. These people. Everything! He felt limp, as if something inside him, inside his spinal column had snapped, forcing his entire nervous system to collapse. Sudden chills -- cold arctic shivers – attacked him, running from his head down to his toes. If only there was work to do, take his mind off things. But the only work available was those humiliating porter jobs... *We work hard for bologna...so hard for bologna...* Cleaning toilets and urinals or going down to the kitchen to listen to the barked commands of sub literate CO's and their grovelling kitchen hands was not for him. So in the absence of constructive work, Peter focused once again on reading and writing and praying.

Dear God, I pray not that the road would be unperilous – we've gone a considerable way beyond that now -- but that I would persevere to the end. Like the little chick in Igbo mythology that was

carried off by the kite in Chinua Achebe's "Things Fall Apart", my cry
is not for help but for the world to know that I am finished

31

Two days to go.

Peter woke up with a start. It was about 4.15 am. He couldn't remember how long he had been dreaming, or whether in fact he had been awake all along but had been in a state of mind without proper perception of reality -- a series of fantastic dream like sequences in his waking brain. All he remembered was having a total visual mental impression, a very clear, vivid picture in his mind – like a neon sign – blinking the message "go to trial". In the background a phantasm of faces, smiling and nodding encouragingly at him...*Juliet, Priscilla, Josh, Gina, Mick, Zik, Chu, Karen, Dobson, Kant, Kiekergaard...the BVM? Or is that you Mom?*

Every nerve in his body, every instinct, every cell, every fibre was transmitting impulses and sensations between his brain and his spinal cord that seemed to be in complete agreement. Feelings of assurance, bravery and audacious calm in danger were so strong. Peter felt inspired, like a mighty spirit was calling him to do his bidding. Not just for him Peter but for all those who had been trampled upon by the... *persecutors!*

So far the spirits of the evil malignant beings had appeared to be winning. The bond hearing…the media circus…the denial of various motions…the mischievously energetic forces of darkness coming together every step of the way, blocking his path.

But after he woke up that morning, somehow Peter was no longer afraid, or angry, or bitter. Exhausted in body, streaking ahead in spirit. Like the prophets of old fearlessly volunteering to be sent on some daunting prophetic mission by God, Peter felt like he had been overtaken by a large and comprehensive essence. Suddenly his existence resonated with meaning. He no longer felt the sense of grim resignation. His spirit soared and he became fearless and free. He was no longer afraid of anything. He had seen the beast and it was no match. A new fire and zeal and defiance kindled in him. His body felt taut with excitement.

Somewhere in the background -- or was it the dim recesses of his mind throwing things up again -- he could hear voices raised in song. There was always some form of raised voice at Queensgate – if it wasn't some kid doing a rap solo, it was the guard barking or inmates shouting at each other or the bible class singing gospel songs – all this in your face before sunrise. *The lunatic currently lives down the hall, but he's petitioning, making furtive application to move into my head!*

32

THE NIGHT BEFORE!

The whole day Peter had confined himself within his confinement. He stayed to himself and read. No visitors! No TV! Although he couldn't help hearing it as it blared away.

"A new report shows the American prison population has risen by seventy seven percent in the last decade...made up of primarily African Americans, Hispanics and Native Americans..."

The poor thought Peter. Those who do not have the funds to hire the best and most appropriate legal assistance, who could not afford the Pit Bull but were stuck with the likes of the Cadaver.

Peter twisted and turned on his rack, trying to bend time to his will, failing. His mind flashed back. In a few years he had become one of the most famous African newscasters and with it had come unimaginable vulnerability. It was like living in a pressure cooker. The spectacular rise and horrendous fall of Peter the Great! Fame and pressure, blowing up simultaneously in his face. People he hadn't spoken to in years, hadn't even heard of, suddenly closing in on him. People who didn't care what kind of person he really was, spreading ugly rumours, accusing him with hurtful intent. People without the benefit of facts, brutal in their hideousness, spinning his life into a very sad, ugly thing.

Peter slept! Strange dreams tormented him. Fear possessed him, benumbing his senses. He felt as if some vile animating essence had taken possession of his body, while his mind watched in horror from behind as it trudged along under extra terrestrial command.

Then a sudden irregular fluctuation, a transmitted noise signal from behind. Peter turned around sharply. A figure stood there, unrecognisable in Virgilian robes, causing him to utter a scream.

Then a voice! A man's voice, familiar, deep, calm and steady.

"Peter *nwa dike* – Peter son of the brave". The voice belonged to Josh. He was speaking to Peter in Igbo, the language of his fathers.

"We believe in you but you must also believe in yourself. Then the ancestral spirits will set you free".

As he spoke, an African rooster crowed.

"Listen to the voice of the rooster", Josh intoned. "*Ko-ko-ro-koo*, it said, not *Cock-a-doodle-doo*".

Josh emerged from the shadows and placed his hand gently on Peter's shoulder. Tears of gratitude rushed out of Peter's eyes. His confidence rose. Then he awoke and the last remnants of his fear vanished.

A minute later the day broke and the loudspeaker crackled into life, barking commands. It was time to prepare for court. Peter felt tired and sleepy but his mind was relaxed and alert.

That strange man had once again given him strength and ammunition -- the indispensable, fundamental absolutely necessary power that would make it possible for him to hold out to the last, to oppose and resist to the bitter end his persecutors, his jailers, his tormentors, those who were causing him severe suffering. This being Josh, who by a series of inexplicable coincidences had entered his life, had transformed his very existence and was now supplying him with those spiritual, philosophical truths like projectiles that he would use to fight back against the predacious instincts of the animals who were ranged against him. Somehow this man or being or extra-terrestrial had given him a blue print for survival, this unbelievable power that was now surging through him, this extraordinary faith and belief in himself that he could take on them and win.

Just before departing for court Peter almost lost his cool. It was as if the pressures of the last 2 months in captivity had reached a head. A sudden fury had taken over him as the guards pushed and prodded and probed and searched.   He had a mad urge to lash out at the entire despicable gang of Corrections Officers. He found their tendency to violate the rights of the inmates galling.

At one stage he shouted and cursed. Two or three guards, Peter could not be sure how many, pounced on him, forcing his hands behind his back and cuffing him very tightly. As they pushed him onto the mobile cage, one of the guards, a stupid looking fellow with a big nose who reminded Peter of a large baboon said: "You can report us to the Queen". His colleagues hooted with laughter. Peter choked with hate.

"I am innocent" he muttered to himself "and should be innocent until proven guilty". But he held back. It wasn't worth fighting for. He had not committed a crime. A crime had been committed against him. He would hold out for the bigger prize. He would relieve them of any power they held over him. By the end of the day, God willing, he would be experiencing the rush of victory.

PART THREE

(Delapsis Resurgum: When I Fall I Shall Rise)

THE JUSTICE CENTRE *REVISITED*

COURTROOM NUMBER SEVEN, IN the heart of the Justice Centre. The scene of Peter's show trial was as busy as a beehive. Temporary platforms had been set up for the battery of cameras and equipment. Wires criss-crossed the floor. Journalists and technicians and cameramen rushed around checking equipment. Court officials made endless trips to the judges' chambers.

Peter was led out for all to see, surrounded as usual by the type of security normally reserved for dangerous criminals. The central figures, made up of the prosecutors, the defence team and Peter "the villain", then occupied the central area.

The prosecutors seemed to Peter to be wearing a festive air, as if they were preparing to celebrate his ignominious downfall, the collapse of the world of Peter the Rascally Rogue, who had been captured and was about to be hung on a tree. *Freak show! Come, one and all!*

Peter regarded his own team. Dobson, his defender, into whose hands he had commended his life, looking rich and TV ready in his thousand-dollar worsted grey suit...*just another shark in a suit...*laughing with some journalist or other.

Tee hee hee hee hee, guffed the fat journo!

Ha haw haw haw haw, came Dobson's boisterous, coarse reply!

What on earth was he guffawing about? Flashing those incisors that had pointed ends like spears and those massive premolars that looked like broad-bladed hoes. The kind of fearless fangs one might find on a witchdoctor's mask. Set against his wide mouth.

Dobson was clearly the New World grinning type – the kind Peter resented, especially when this particular grinning type was being paid a substantial sum not to grin but to get him out of this hell. But no! Instead, hot shot here seemed to find something to guff about after each failure – and let's face it, Peter thought with a stab of resentment, every step of the way so far he had failed, hadn't he? Failed to reduce the bond, failed to sustain any motions. Yet he found something to chuckle about with some journo. And now with Karen, the other rather more attractive looking half of his legal dream team, with her neatly coiffed hair and yes…bright grin! *I hate my place in the world right now and all you can do is grin. What have I become to you?*

Both Karen and Dobson seemed really excited by the media attention, Peter noted resentfully. You could see it in their faces, how they relished the glory at his expense. Taking zestful pleasure at the idea of a showdown on camera. *Let's get ready to ru-m-m-b-le!* Blissfully happy to be handling the most talked about case, to have their smug grinning mugs on television and in the newspapers, already calculating the benefits from such a celebrated trial. Free advert, potential clients and the greenbacks they could have coming, whether they won or lost, as a result of his misfortune. *My corpse that they have desecrated lies as carrion for you to feast on!*

It wouldn't be long now before the judge emerged and the games began. A chance for Dobson to cease grinning and earn his pay, making those sanctimonious, self-righteous *persecutors* choke on their travesties.

Tension mounted. The courtroom was swallowed up in silence, waiting for the judge whose entrance was imminent. A few officials lolled around. Time, shrouded in a dark cloud, crawled past. Anxiety kicked at Peter's heart, jolting it into palpitation. In the public area, there was a low, almost imperceptible hum of voices, rising and falling lightly.

At last, Judge Burrows, a tall bespectacled sexagenarian dressed in black robes, emerged and mounted his bench. The hum subsided and so did the drumming of Peter's heart. He realised looking around the courtroom at the press, the prosecutors and the police, that they had done their worst. They couldn't hurt him anymore.

Judge Burrows brought his gavel down. Let the battle begin!

Jury selection! From a jury pool of around 20, eight white women, three white men and one black woman, were selected.

The trial! Dobson was absolutely superbly brilliant. So systematic, thorough, confident and calm. Destroyed *the woman* and her tainted testimony on the stand. Restored Peter's shaken confidence in lawyers. At one stage he had even thought of firing him. Peter was especially glad he didn't!

Dobson's performance was captivating. He was a master of his art and he held centre stage. Peter could see the jury was riveted. It wasn't so much the logic of his approach. Nor was it just the clarity of his thought, though these were much in evidence. It was more than that.   It was the style of it all that left everyone breathless. *What you say is nothing. How you say it is everything.*

Peter could feel relief washing over him as Dobson worked the jury, putting doubts away, filling Peter's tortured bruised soul with confidence and hope.

By evening, much of the tide of negative media had turned. Reporters across the five local terrestrial TV channels were almost unanimous in predicting that Peter was going to win and that the prosecutor's case had broken down irretrievably.

In the latest twist in the trial by media of our fallen colleague, having examined all the evidence presented in court and having ourselves tried and failed to bury him, we have no choice but to find him INNOCENT of the crime and to award today's round of the courtroom championship to the Mighty Pit Bull! Things could of course change tomorrow...the prosecution could pull a surprise out of a hat...a "hat trick of three wickets" I think the English call it.

Heh! Heh!Heh! Heh! Heh! chortled the presenter.

Peter was sitting with Ried in the television area, using the remote to flick through various versions of the local evening news. For the first time since his incarceration he was finally getting a glimpse of justice – just a glimpse -- and he felt confident enough to watch his own trial, or the way *they* were interpreting his trial. On-the-scene journalists were broadcasting live from the Justice Centre. Behind them, Peter could see a forest of remote transmit-

ters sticking out of the tops of Outside Broadcast vans. Down at
the bottom cables as thick as boa constrictors twisted around each
other like huge mangrove vines, carrying electrical impulses that
before his very eyes metamorphosed into the faces and voices on
the screen, announcing the end of the first round of the contest
and awarding victory to the Pit Bull. *Switching sides without so
much as a sad face!* Local television stars scrambled to anchor "the
big story", amusing Peter with their antics. Did these people really have any formal journalistic training or were they all amateur
actors?

Flick! There's that bleach blonde all-American tosser with a
voice like an agitated beehive. *Flick!* There's that old bat from
channel 9, attempting to put on an unscripted performance,
bombing seriously, direly. *Flick!* And there's that pregnant woman
– pretty, trendy mother-to-be -- What's her face? Kristi something
or other.

Of the lot, Peter's favourite quip clip came from that mop-
haired reporter on Channel 5, Nick Botsford, who announced
that "the legs had literally been cut off of the prosecutions case".
Nick had taken the time to put together a considered package,
examining the evidence piece by piece, tearing the prosecution's
case to shreds. That night, Peter slept comfortably for the first
time since his incarceration.

After the excitement and delays of the first day, the second day
was much smoother. The pace was more relaxed and Dobson was
even better. His voice was loud, lucid and confident, winning
fresh converts among the jurors and the press. The prosecutors
on the other hand were dull and uninspiring. Their case was
clearly full of holes. They had been so certain of victory. They
never even bothered to prepare, just as Dobson had predicted.
The mighty Pit Bull had once again reduced their argument to
absurdity. *Reductum absurdum* Peter thought with a smile, as his
Latin began to come back.

Peter turned his attention to the prosecuting attorney who had come in place of the chief prosecutor. He was a red faced, upright walking, giant beetle called Larry. He had a heavy spherical head like a large beetroot and shaggy, scowling eyebrows projecting out of his forehead, overhanging dull eyes and a bulbous organ containing two nostrils that made Peter think of the open end of a nozzle or a pair of bellows. A vertical groove like a glyph carved a pathway downwards from his fleshy nose, broadening out at the end into two slices of raw meat, which puckered into a wrinkled contraction that could pass for an exceedingly thin, cruel mouth. His huge hands seemed made for ramming, crushing and driving wedges. One reckless hit from those things could permanently alter the shape of a man's skull. He had on a cheap navy suit, a white shirt with a dirty neckline and a yellow tie with black polka dots. So shabby and unprofessional next to the spiffy Pit Bull! His cross-examination lacked teeth and pretty soon, when it emerged that he had no idea the *woman* had also been having an affair with Peter's elder brother Zik, it became clear he was struggling to maintain credibility as well as hold the attention of the jurors. Sometimes Peter felt as if he was talking about someone else, not him.

In the middle of it all, Dobson made another one of his seemingly sudden decisions. He decided he didn't want Peter to testify. He felt the case had been well presented, including Peter's objections that Peter had written down and passed to him on the first day of the trial and he did not want to run the risk of Peter making mistakes on the stand.

Peter was disappointed. He had looked forward to having his day in court. But Dobson seemed to know what he was doing and Peter reluctantly accepted his decision.

33

WAITING FOR THE JURY to complete their deliberations was the nightmare to end all nightmares, filled with haunting obsessive suffocating fear. It was worse than anything Peter could have ever imagined. Sitting there, waiting, hearing screaming, rushing sounds in his head, feeling sudden jets of blind panic shooting in and out of him, making hissing noises in his mind's ear as they came and went, forcing him to gasp for air. Ghastly images forming in his head. What if…what if…?

Peter gnawed at his fingernails nervously. He was sitting across from Dobson in a large waiting area with rows of bolted down chairs and tables. It was one flight of stairs up from the courtroom and the jury room where they were deciding his fate. A room inhabited by Corrections officers, lawyers and their clients. Awaiting that final word…actually Peter hoped for final *words* rather than word. Whatever happened, it must not be single…on its own…one word! Because that could only mean one thing and that one thing for Peter was too frightening to contemplate.

"So what happens now?" Peter asked Dobson apprehensively. "Just wait?"

"That's right", Dobson replied evenly. "Wait and think positive. I can't see how a jury can possibly convict you after hearing that suspicious testimony from her".

Peter nodded. That would make sense based on what he had seen in court. But in the final stages that judge – Burrows or whatever he was called – had scared Peter. He seemed to be summing up in a way that emphasised guilty rather than not guilty. And that Jury – all white bar one. And most of them women! How could they be a jury of his peers? What was that nut Dobson thinking when he picked them? *What chance do I have with that lot?*

After about half an hour, an officer, going bald and inclining to fat, announced that the jurors had summoned the court. Peter rose slowly, aware of his throbbing heart, feeling like his legs were made of jelly.

It turned out to be a false alarm. The jurors wanted some clarification: Did the state have an obligation to record and send decisions of judges in such cases to the respondent?

Come on folks, thought Peter. I live in a foreign country. How else would I know the judges decision?

Shortly afterwards, they were called back again for another question: Could the particular felony with which Peter was charged be read out to them again?

A few minutes later, Peter was told the jury had reached a verdict and was led back into the courtroom. It had taken just over an hour. He was keenly aware of the drumming beat of his heart. He sat there shivering, staring the terrible prospect and consequence of a guilty verdict in the face, an earthquake of a shudder suddenly running the course of his body.

The jury door opened and you could have heard a pin drop. As the men and women who held his fate in their hands slowly filed back into the courtroom, Peter's heart lurched dangerously and seemed to slip from its usual place just under his sternum into free fall. Down, down, down! Peter could now feel it banging madly against his ribs. Or was that his solar plexus? And something else – anxiety -- was rooting around in his lower belly, in the pit of his alimentary canal, in a complex of radiating nerves, threatening him with incontinence, paralysing his limbs.

Peter tried to ignore it, concentrating on searching the juror's faces for clues. Nothing! They all looked poker faced. Worse! They wouldn't look in his direction, but kept their eyes averted, trained on Judge Burrows' bench.

The foreman, passing something...a white bit of paper to Judge Burrows.

The judge, his eyes lowered, hooded, reading it.

The court, silent, frozen. Then the moment!

"Ladies and Gentlemen of the jury, have you reached a verdict?"

"Yes, your honour".

"In the matter of the state of Ohio versus Peter Oti, how do you find the defendant?"

"*Not* guilty, your honour".

"And how have you reached that verdict?"

"By unanimous decision, your honour".

The red-faced prosecutor staring bug-eyed first at the judge then at the jury, his mouth agape with dismay, too shocked for words, eyes aflame in a red haze, a mad look on his face. Stunned and smouldering with anger, crushed by Dobson.

Meanwhile, commotion breaking out in the courtroom... cheers coming from the public gallery... The jurors smiling at Peter now, slowly filing out...Peter looking dazed...Dobson nudging him sharply, whispering urgently. "Thank the jury, thank the jury". "Thank you", Peter croaked, his voice trembling, the tears finally coming in great cascading falls.

The shield of winter had been broken and spring was about to strike.

Peter could live again.

EPILOGUE

Nine months later…

Dear Josh,

I hope this letter reaches you because let's face it, I don't have an official address for you. Even if I did, I'm not sure it would be on the postman's map. So I'm sending it to Queensgate.

Sorry its taken me this long to write. As the Igbo people of Nigeria say, I have not found the mouth with which to tell of my plight till now. If I had seen my life in a movie I would not have believed it.

For the first time since my troubles ended nine months ago and I arrived back in England, I am experiencing happiness and relief. My life, which had altered so fundamentally, seems to be getting back to normal again and the horrors of the past few months are gradually receding.

After my release, I walked down the streets of Cincinnati with my brother Chu, relishing my freedom, feeling like my old self again. Two days later, I left Cincinnati for London and the waiting arms of my Juliet. I shall probably return to Cinti someday, although that is the last thing on my mind now.

So do I hate my persecutors? Those who very nearly destroyed my life? I have to admit that for a while I did. I wanted to hate them and hit them and hurt them. I wanted to keep all the rage. But in the end, I let most of it go. Not for their sake, but for mine and for my daughters because I want us to live a happy life.

But I think I am still angry with the chief prosecutor for the evil he wanted to do to me, for sensationalising my life, turning it into a monstrous drama. When I think of it, I get quite emotional. I even cry sometimes.

The important thing is that the terrible months finally dragged to a close. I have faith in the Great Spirit and all the things you taught me.

Thanks for everything! I look forward to meeting you again in higher Spirituality!

Your friend

Peter

Golders Green, North West London, April 2001

POST SCRIPT

PETER OTI NEVER SAW or heard from Josh again.

In November 2002, Peter was reinstated as a casual business and world news presenter on CNN International.

After six months, the shifts dried up. But, as a result of his exposure on CNNI, Peter was offered various independent, commercial and corporate television production projects. He subsequently created his own television production company.

After a few years making a series of acclaimed documentaries and infomercials, Peter steered the company fully into movie production and became a highly regarded producer and director in Africa and Europe.

To this day, although he insists he will make the trip sometime soon, he has not returned to the United States.